Aging & Ministry in the 21st Century

Aging & Ministry in the 21st Century

An Inquiry Approach

Richard H. Gentzler, Jr., D.Min.

DISCIPLESHIP RESOURCES

PO BOX 340003 • NASHVILLE, TN 37203-0003
www.discipleshipresources.org

AGING & MINISTRY IN THE 21st CENTURY: An Inquiry Approach. Copyright © 2008 Discipleship Resources. Discipleship Resources ® and design logos are trademarks owned by Discipleship Resources, a ministry of GBOD ®, Nashville, Tennessee. All rights reserved. No part of this book may be reproduced in any form whatsoever, print or electronic, without written permission. For information regarding rights and permissions, contact Discipleship Resources, P.O. Box 340003, Nashville TN 37203-0003; fax 615-340-1789.

ISBN 978-0-88177-540-2

Library of Congress Cataloging-in-Publication Data

Gentzler, Richard H.
  Aging & ministry in the 21st century : an inquiry approach / Richard
H. Gentzler, Jr.
       p. cm.
  Includes bibliographical references.
  ISBN 978-0-88177-540-2
  1. Church work with older people. I. Title. II. Title: Aging and
ministry in the 21st century.
  BV4435.G44 2008
  259'.3--dc22
                              2008024844

SPECIAL THANKS

To Teri Kline for her encouragement, support, and dedication to the GBOD's Center on Aging & Older Adult Ministries, to Sandy Zeigler for her caring persistence in seeing that this book is published, to editors George Donigian and Terrie Livaudais, who perfected this book with patient and masterful editing skills.

Contents

Introduction

Why should the church be concerned with older adult ministries? Aren't we being short-sighted by expanding our time and energy in ministry with older adults? After all, shouldn't the time and energy of the church be better spent in children's, youth, and young adult ministries? Aren't young people the future of the church?

Perhaps, you, too, have similar questions and concerns as you begin reading this book. Maybe you are a pastor who has been appointed or called to a congregation with many older members and you are bewildered about knowing how to begin a ministry with older adults. Or, perhaps your church is thinking about starting an older adult ministry and your pastor has asked you to coordinate the efforts of a team. Maybe you are caring for an older person and you want to know more about his or her specific needs. Possibly you feel called into this special and vital ministry, and simply want to know more about older adult ministries. One thing is for sure, you have opened yourself up to God's leading. God is present with you in your reading, reflecting, and sharing. God is concerned about older adults, both their temporal world as well as their eternal salvation. As a leader, you play a vital role in the well-being of older adults. Now, I invite you to allow the Holy Spirit to set your learning and experience in its proper, larger context of formation and service.

You probably already know that the older adult population is growing both in our society and in most of our congregations. We are poised on the brink of a "longevity revolution." People are living longer, healthier lives thanks in part to public health advances and medical research breakthroughs. The graying of the huge Baby Boom generation during the coming decades will amplify this fact with more than one in five Americans being over the age of 65.

Likewise, in many of our congregations, we are seeing our fastest growth in our older adult memberships. Older adults fill our pews, provide for our financial stability, and participate in learning and service opportunities. Sometimes they are the gatekeepers in our churches. Other times, they are the keepers of tradition. Occasionally, they are the not so silent voices of despair, discouragement, and discontent. But, they are also always in need of faith formation and renewal.

Keep in mind, the future of the church is in the hands of our older adults. That's right. The future really isn't in the hands of children or young people, although the church often suggests such platitudes. I invite you to think about this with me for a moment. The large numbers and importance of older adults in our congregations are clearly felt in at least four areas of church life: leadership, presence, gifts, and service.

Older adults provide leadership in our congregations. They are often our bishops, pastors, and lay volunteers in our churches. They serve in leadership roles on our boards, committees, teams, and councils. They teach in our Sunday schools, serve as lay leaders and lay speakers, make church policy and often control the church budget. They are passing on the traditions and values of the Christian faith by preaching the word, teaching the Scriptures, and sharing their stories with others. They are demonstrating Christ's love as mentors, teachers, and leaders.

When congregations decide to start a new Bible study program or group, often older adults are present to participate in the new venture. Older adults are also present in our pews on Sunday mornings, Sunday evenings, and weeknight services. They participate in Sunday school classes and in other study groups. In many of our churches, older adults have a larger proportion of membership than other age cohorts. They are often the first to sign up, the first to attend, the first to invite, the first to welcome, and the last to leave.

It is generally believed that older adults give a higher percentage of their income to the church and are considered the most generous givers in their faith community. Studies have shown that younger generations do not contribute to religious institutions as generously as do their elders. Sometimes older adults are viewed as controlling the "purse strings" in a church and are more cautious about spending. This attitude may be due to their upbringing and to the economy (the Depression) when they were young. However, the gifts of older adults are often of vital importance to the financial well-being of local churches.

While young women and men may be engaged in raising a family, completing their education, and establishing themselves in a career, older adults have the time to serve the needs of their congregation and community. Older adults want to feel useful. They need to be needed. They want to experience a sense of meaning, and they want to make a significant difference in the lives of others. Many older adults provide necessary and vital assistance as volunteers in community service and local mission projects. Some are engaged in short term mission opportunities throughout our nation and the world. Older adults have the time and practical knowledge (wisdom) gained from years of experience. They often have the energy and drive to want to make a difference through their service to others.

For these reasons and many others, the future of our congregations is in the hands of older adults, for they help shape and mold the church's ministry by their leadership, presence, gifts, and service. May we incline our hearts and minds to the words of the psalmist who proclaimed: "In old age they still produce fruit; they are always green and full of sap" (Psalm 92:14). Older adults have much to give to the church, not least of which is the sharing of their wisdom, faith, and experience. If we want to revitalize the church today, older adults must be included in our vision. If we fail to reach, nurture, and equip older adults for Christian service, the church will lose the wealth of experience, wisdom, and faith that often abounds with older adults.

Using this Book

Aging and Ministry in the 21st Century is designed to encourage and facilitate a formative experience for you. You will learn much about the aging process and the developmental stage of older adulthood. You will also learn new ways of helping your congregation develop an intentional and comprehensive ministry by, with, and for older adults.

As you work through this study, you will find various exercises that will guide you to personal reflection. Some of the exercises will be easy and fun. Others, you may find more difficult and challenging. Yet I believe this phase of your study will yield some meaningful impression that will help guide you in your ministry.

You may also spend time in group study. Obviously, group experiences vary widely. Your individual experience will depend upon the group leadership, other participants, class setting, and a host of other variables, as well as your own experience and interest in this ministry. There are, however, some guidelines you will want to keep in mind, whether you read this book on your own or as part of a larger group study.

First, have an attitude for learning. Desire to learn from others. When you are in the group setting you will want to contribute, to learn, and to grow. A spirit of humility should characterize each member of the group. We are all students learning what it means to age faithfully and how we can be intentional in older adult ministry. No one person has all the answers, holds all the truth, or has all the knowledge. Aging is a life-long process and pretending that we know everything older adults need or want is not only presumptuous but also futile.

Second, if you are leading a group, do not talk too much. No one person should monopolize the group discussion. Everyone is encouraged to share their ideas and experiences. A good group is like an orchestra; each instrument serves the whole and adds to the overall performance.

Third, be open to sharing your own experience. Vital groups encourage individual members to share their own experiences, both successes and failures, related to ministry with older adults. This may even include raising sensitive or controversial subject matter. Openly sharing ideas can be a way of learning from one another and can have an impact on the way older adult ministry is eventually realized in a particular setting.

Finally, be a good steward of time. Passion is one thing. Misguided enthusiasm is another. Be respectful of the class time. It may seem natural to want to exceed your allotted class time when things are really going well. But to evolve into a group that does not know when to stop can be destructive to the learning process. The old adage that it is better to end too soon than too late applies to healthy groups. It is better to leave wanting more than to leave feeling overloaded!

What You Will Study

In addition the Introductory section, this book is divided into eight chapters or class sessions. Each chapter is designed to help the student move deeper into a comprehensive and intentional ministry by, with, and for older adults.

Myths, realities, and aging is the focus of Chapter 1. You will read and reflect on common misconceptions about aging and the stereotypes that permeate much of our society and are present in most of our congregations. We will look at who are the older adults in our churches and the aging experience in today's world.

Health and aging is the primary emphasis of Chapter 2. We will explore physiological changes of aging. Understanding the need for fitness and healthy lifestyles will also be addressed in this chapter. Issues of cognitive aging will be shared, too.

In Retirement and Aging, Chapter 3, we will explore the changes in retirement in our society. In particular, we will look at the changing face of retirement, the three phases of retirement, and managing retirement. Also, we will discuss the church's role in ministry with persons in the retirement years.

Spirituality and aging is the topic of Chapter 4. Learning about the faith needs of older adults, as well as religious participation in later life, will be emphasized in this chapter. In addition, grief and loss and end-of-life issues will be explored.

Chapter 5 is titled Caregiving and Aging. We will profile caregivers and explore trends related to caregiving. We will also discuss ways congregations can be intentional in their caregiving ministry. Elder abuse will also be explored. A growing reality in our society is that increasing numbers of grandparents are raising grandchildren. We will explore this phenomenon and the role the church can play in this important issue.

The topics of death and end-of-life planning are found in Chapter 6. Learning about our societal view of death and dying as well as the biblical understanding of death is provided for the reader. Advance directives are discussed in the section on end-of-life planning.

Ministry and Aging is the title of Chapter 7. This is a "how-to" section of our study. Developing a comprehensive, intentional ministry with older adults will be explored as we learn how to get started in this vital ministry. Also, organizational development and the role of leadership will be lifted up.

Finally, Chapter 8 takes a look at Boomers and Aging. The baby boom generation numbers approximately 77 million and is fast becoming the leading edge in the older adult population. In 1864, Robert Browning penned his famous lines about aging, "Grow old along with me! The best is yet to be, the last of life, for which the first was made." The Boomer generation may be in a position to make these words a reality as they experience the changing effects of an aging society.

You will also find a helpful resource section at the end of the book. An annotated bibliography of books, videos, and websites is made available for further insight, information, and reference. In addition, various forms and survey materials are supplied in the Appendix section to help assist you in your ministry.

Myths, Realities, and Aging

Not all older adults are alike. Diversity is a good word that best describes the older adult population, for this group is remarkably heterogeneous. While there are some similarities in experiences that older adults share, no two older adults are exactly alike. Each age, gender, race, and ethnic group has distinctive characteristics, and the experience of every older adult is unique.

Older adults are often lumped together and labeled as "old." Most people have met 85-year-olds they would describe as "young" as well as 45-year-olds they would characterize as "old." In other words, a 75-year-old woman may be "younger" than a 60-year-old man; she may be healthier, have more energy, and may even be working, while never having had a major illness. Whereas, the 60-year-old man may be inactive, be vulnerable to cardiovascular disease, and be disengaged from social interactions. Recognizing the differences in aging experiences is extremely important for leaders of older adult ministry.

It is also important for us to recognize some of our thinking about aging and old age is not based on fact. Several myths about the aging adult must be unlearned. They are only half-truths at best; unfounded and inappropriately generalized for such a large and diverse population. One myth is that older adults are frail and end their lives in nursing homes. This could not be further from the truth. Older adults are in better health today than ever before. In fact, at any given time, less than 5% of people over age 65 are in long-term care settings.

Another myth is that older adults are not interested in learning new things.

When you scan the experiences of an 85-year-old man or a 95-year-old woman, you will quickly discover that throughout their lives, they have been learning new things. Think about all the changes that have happened in the lives of most 85-year-old men and 95-year-old women! Such changes brought about opportunities for learning new ideas, new techniques, and new innovations and technologies. Today, with the success of the Elderhostel movement, community college classes, and a variety of other learning settings, including many Sunday school classes, older adults are taking the opportunity to learn new things. From exploring the internet to the mission fields of Tibet, older adults are engaging themselves in learning more about themselves and the world in which they live.

Still another myth is that older people as they age, become more alike. How could they be? They have had more time to be different from each other than any other age group. In fact, the more people age, the less alike they become. After 70, 80, or 90 years of living, people develop their own highly personal ways of thinking and feeling, behaving, and coping. Their bodies have also been shaped by a long history of contending with the world. As a result, people differ widely in their personal and social needs, their reactions to illness and to treatment, their spiritual development, their desires and goals, and their styles of living.

Yet what is the first impression you have when you think of an older woman? An older man? Let me invite you reflect on the following two questions:

1. What are the first three words or phrases that come into your mind when you visualize an older woman?

_____

_____

_____

2. What are the first three words or phrases that come into your mind when you visualize an older man?

_____

_____

_____

Now analyze what you have written. Does what you have written hold true for all older women, and for all older men? Do you believe that your words or phrases are an accurate description of all older women and older men or only of some older women and older men? Why or why not? Getting in touch with your own myths and stereotypes is important for the success of your ministry.

Teach Me To Grow Old

I once heard a devout Christian say: "All my life I've been taught how to die, but no one ever taught me how to grow old." As people age, they often find role models in short supply. Older adults today are pioneers in aging and what it means to live a long life.

Growing old can be difficult in our culture. The failure of society to prepare us for old age is alarming, considering the increasing elderly population in the United States. Not only do older adults have to deal with financial insecurities, health conditions, loneliness, and role losses, etc., but the prevailing attitude toward older people in our culture can be quite discriminatory. Even the Psalmist had a fear of being rejected in old age, "Do not cast me off in the time of old age; do not forsake me when my strength is spent." (Psalm 71:9)

Our culture argues that aging is an unnatural and immoral imposition on us all. It proclaims that old age means decline and perfection is remaining young. As such, a person's worth is associated with work; and, people are considered worthy as a result of their productivity, beauty, and strength. To loose any of these is to be placed at a decisive disadvantage in society. Therefore, it isn't easy to grow old in our society because how we age often depends on the way we internalize society's images of being old.

I recently heard an old Vietnamese-American woman say, "The old are obsolete here in America. Neither respected nor deemed important. Back home, the elders are given the highest place of honor, and it was they who dispensed wisdom and shared their experiences with those who came up after them. It's not true here. No one wants to hear what you have to say."

Ageism, which is prejudice or discrimination against people because of their age, is particularly pronounced in our society as it reflects beliefs and attitudes related to old age. Fear of aging prevents many people of all ages from seeing that potentials are as bountiful as are problems among older adults. Negative images of older adults are often reflected by the stereotypic oldsters who are the butt of greeting cards and popular jokes. Like "racism" and "sexism," ageism demeans and devalues people.

Unfortunately, ageism is widespread not only in the marketplaces but also in religious circles. We hear words like, "The church is dying because we have so many old people in the church." "If old people would just get out of the way." "If older adults just accepted change." "Either older adults should get with the program or they should leave the church." As a result of such attitudes, ageism often causes congregations to neglect the spiritual and emotional needs of older adults.

Ageism is manifested in our society's worship of youth and our anxiety over gray hair and wrinkles. Such attitude diminishes the church's witness and mission. When older adults see little interest directed at them by the church, they gradually lose their sense of themselves as having value and worth, which dampens and diminishes their faith development.

Let me ask you a question: If on a particular Sunday morning, you have visiting your church a young family (father, mother, and children) and on that same Sunday, you have an older couple or widow visiting your church, do you extend as much energy reaching the older couple or widow as you do the young family? If not, why? Is the older couple or widow of any less importance to God? Is the presence of the older couple or widow of less value to your congregation and ministry?

> What evidences of ageism have you become aware of in your local church? Explain.
>
> _____
>
> _____
>
> _____
>
> How might an intentional ministry by, with, and for older adults make a difference in the life of your church?
>
> _____
>
> _____
>
> _____

Ageism often occurs when church leaders do not listen to the desires of older adults but assume that they know what older adults need. Such an attitude causes congregations to neglect the spiritual and emotional needs of older adults. As a result, ageism is a major factor working against joyful, vital ministry with older adults.

It is vital for church leaders who are engaged in ministry with older adults to get in touch with their own aging. It is next to impossible to be an effective leader with older adults if we are not in touch with our own aging. As you reflect on aging and growing old, I invite you to reflect personally on what aging means to you. Take a few moments and think about the following question;

1. What does aging mean to you personally?

    A. Decline
    B. Dependency
    C. Disability
    D. Disease
    E. All of Above
    F. None of the Above

Why do you imagine aging as you do? _____

_____

_____

2. Regardless of your present age, how do you feel about getting older?

_____

_____

3. Do you have fears about growing old? _____ If "yes," name them.

_____

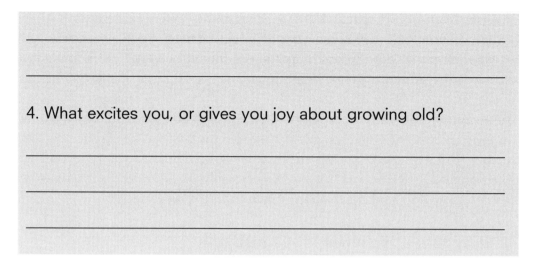

4. What excites you, or gives you joy about growing old?

Being in ministry with older adults can be a deeply rewarding and challenging experience. But it is important for each of us to get in touch with our own aging before we can expect to be effective in ministry with older adults.

Who Are Older Adults?

Who are the older adults who live in our communities and worship in our churches? A quick response would be people who are:

- Healthy and active
- Transitionally impaired (e.g., as a result of the death of a significant loved one, a devastating health condition, or some other major "interruption" in life)
- Homebound
- Frail
- Institutionalized (in nursing homes, hospitals, prisons)
- Dying
- Married
- Always Single
- Widowed
- Divorced
- Remarried

But, of course, these are not the only descriptors for older adults. Others include, primary caregivers, grandparents raising grandchildren, college students (yes, there are older adults in college), employed full-time, employed part-time, retired, and volunteers. In other words, the list is endless. For every older adult, there are a variety of descriptors. Think about the older adults you know and the many roles they fulfill in their own life.

What are other roles or descriptors for older adults that you can name?

Defining and Describing Aging in Later Life

Aging is not a single event but a process that begins at birth, ends at death, and occurs at different rates and in different ways for all people. In other words, no two people age exactly alike. Aging, in fact, is a very individual process.

Classifying a person as "old," depends on whom you ask and what you measure. The simplest index is age; but that is not a satisfactory measure in individual cases. Aging is a continuum and not easily described. We can each think of people who are "old" or "young" for their age. It all depends on how they go through the aging process.

In general, an older adult is defined as anyone who is 65-years of age or older. In the future, this view may change as longevity increases. Other terms, such as elderly or seniors, are also commonly used to describe this population. Throughout this book, you will find all three terms used interchangeably.

There are several key principles for defining and describing aging and later life.

Chronological age is used by many public programs to define age groups. Until recently, in the United States eligibility for full Social Security benefits came at age 65. Presently, mandatory retirement age for clergy in The United Methodist Church is 70 years of age. These are just two examples of describing later life by chronological age.

Social age is when social positions create images of older adults in people's minds. Words like: retiree, widow, and nursing home resident create certain images about the lifestyle of older adults.

Functional age is determined by what people can do. In functional terms, people become older when they can no longer perform the major roles of adulthood. Functional age may also be measured by such normal physical changes as stiffness of joints or decreased skin elasticity.

Subjective age is how old people feel. One person may be 75 and feel young while a 55-year-old may feel old. Often the perception of when people become old shifts by age group. To a 10-year-old, a college student may seem old; but to a 90-year-old, an 80-year-old may seem young.

It is also important to keep in mind that older adults have basic needs just like people of all ages. Older adults need to be respected, valued, and loved. They want to be remembered and to have purpose and meaning in their life. Erik Erikson, a social psychologist, wrote that older adults have a need to give something back to succeeding generations (which he labeled, Generativity) and George Vaillant, medical doctor, wrote that older adults have a desire to preserve traditions (which he labeled, Keepers of the Meaning). Information regarding the developmental tasks of older adults is valuable for church leaders as they understand and help support the desire of older adults through the third and fourth quarters of their lives.

Why Older Adult Ministry?

Why should congregations design intentional ministry by, with, and for older adults?

First, the population of persons aged 65 and over in the United States increased from 3 million in 1900 to 35 million in 2000. The number is expected to reach 55 million by 2020, a 56 percent gain—much faster than the growth projected for the United States population as a whole. By 2030, there will be nearly 72 million people aged 65 and over, an increase of more than 100 percent since 2000. Probably no trend in the last 100 years has had a greater impact on the nature of religious, social, and political life than the dramatic demographic shifts reflected in our growing aging population. The rapid growth in the number of adults in their sixties, seventies, eighties, and even nineties will focus the church's attention on the wants and needs of older members.

Second, the percentage of older adults in the United States is increasing and older adults may soon outnumber both children and youth. In 1900, children and youth made up 40% of the total population in the United States, while only 4% of the population was made up of persons aged 65 and older. But, it is highly likely that by 2030, older adults aged 65 and over will outnumber both children and youth (21% verses 19% respectively). Perhaps even more astonishing is this: Between 2004 and 2020, the number of people in the United States over 50 will grow by 74%, while the number of people under 50 will grow by only 1%. What does it mean for our churches and communities, when older adults have a higher percentage of the population than children and youth?

Third, the average life expectancy in the United States is increasing. The average life expectancy increased from 47 years in 1900 to 77 years in 2000. As a result, more people are living into their eighties and nineties. In 2000, there were a little more than 50,000 centenarians (people 100 and older) in the United States; but, by 2050, it is expected that there will be approximately 1 million centenarians in the United States. Population aging is the result of at least two powerful developments: lower birth rates and longer life spans. Neither of which seem to be abating in the foreseeable future.

Fourth, many of our congregations have a high percentage of older adults as members. In The United Methodist Church, 55% of our membership is 50 years of age and over, while nearly 30% of our membership is 65 years and older. What does it mean for our congregations when so many of our members are older and our churches are "graying?" The United Methodist Church is not alone in this demographic picture—many other denominations, including most "mainline" denominations, are experiencing increasing percentages in the numbers of older members.

Review your church membership. How many members in your church are:

50–64 years of age?_____

65–74 years of age?_____

75–84 years of age?_____

85–94 years of age?_____

95 and older?_____

What percentage of your congregation is comprised of people 65 years of age and older?_____

Our Aging Population

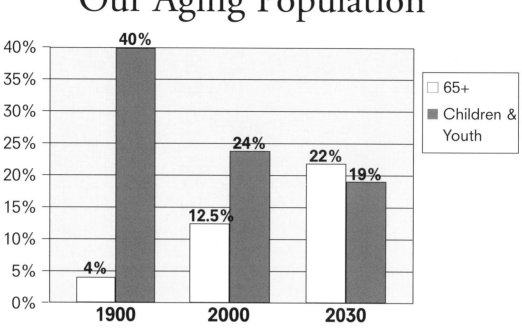

Years

Centenarians

Persons 100 years or older in the US

1950:	4,475
1990:	37,307
2000:	50,454
2050★:	1,100,000

(★Projected. Source: U.S. Census Bureau)

United Methodist Church

55% of membership is 50 years of age or older

Nearly 30% of membership is 65 years of age or older

Fifth, God loves older adults. The Bible is filled with references of God's love for and value in older adults. Several passages are mentioned here:

- "Honor your father and your mother, so that your days may be long in the land that the Lord your God is giving you." (Exodus 20:12)
- "Is wisdom with the aged; and understanding in length of days?" (Job 12:12)
- "Gray hair is a crown of glory; it is gained in a righteous life" (Proverbs 16:31)
- "The glory of youth is their strength, but the beauty of the aged is their gray hair." (Proverbs 20:29)
- "Religion that is pure and undefiled before God, is this: to care for orphans and widows in their distress." (James 1:27)

What other Bible verses or Bible stories can you identify that address issues of old age and older adults?

_____

_____

_____

_____

_____

Finally, and sixth, aging is changing. The age of 65 is no longer the benchmark signaling the onset of late life. As we face the dawn of the 21st Century, we find that people who are now 65 years of age and older generally are healthier, wealthier, and more active than was true of previous elderly cohorts. As the Boomer generation moves into the stage of older adulthood, the difference in aging from previous generations may be dramatic as we will discuss in Chapter 8.

A recent cover of the AARP magazine announced that sixty is the new thirty! With so dramatic a change, the church must move beyond the stereotype of older adult ministry as something done only *for* and *to* the aging. Rather, it is intentional and comprehensive and is ministry *by*, *with*, and *for* older adults.

A pastor told a story once about the importance of older members in the church by using the image of the face on a clock. The pastor pointed out that on a clock face there may be three hands: the second hand, the minute hand, and the hour hand. The pastor likened the second hand to the younger members in the congregation. They have lots of energy and race around doing things, just as the second hand goes all the way around the clock face in just 60 seconds.

The minute hand is like members in the congregation who are a little older, perhaps middle-aged. They don't have quite the energy of the younger members but still accomplish much, just as the minute hand moves slower than the second hand but still gets around the clock face one every hour.

The older members in the congregation are like the hour hand, which moves a lot slower than the second hand or the minute hand but still gets around the clock face every twelve hours. They may have less energy than they once had but they keep moving along at their own pace.

Each hand on the clock has its function. But then the pastor said, "If you had no second hand on the clock, could you tell what time it is? Yes. If you removed the minute hand too and just had the hour hand, could you still tell the time? Yes, not as precisely, but you could make a pretty close guess. But if the clock had only the second hand could you tell the time? No. How about if you had only the minute hand? No. Even if the clock had both the second hand and the minute hand, could you tell what time it is? No. You need the hour hand."

So even though the older members may not be able to keep up the same pace as younger members, they are vital to the spiritual health and continuity of the congregation. They are encouraged to keep doing what they can, at the pace they are able to maintain, for the benefit and blessing of all in the congregation. All members are important in the congregation, from the youngest to the oldest.

Health and Aging

CHAPTER 2

Physiological Changes of Aging

Although our bodies change as we grow older, the health status of an older adult is the result of many factors, including genetics, behavior, lifestyle, and environmental factors. As a result, is it possible to describe "typical" aging or a "typical" older adult? Probably not. When we hear the word "aging," people likely develop images of gray hair, wrinkled skin, diminished lung capacity, stooped posture, cataracts, impaired hearing, and dementia. Yet such a picture is really a caricature of a typical older adult.

This stereotypical image of aging does not hold true for all older adults. Aging is really more complex than that. Older adults age at different rates. A group of older adults that are the same chronological age may be very different from each other in external appearance, behavior, and health conditions. In fact, you may know an 85-year-old church member who may act and appear as young as, or younger than, another older adult who is 65. Recognize that while similarities exist, there are individual differences that must be respected and treated accordingly.

It is important to note that the body does not age all at once or at the same rate. For example, a person can have healthy kidneys but experience heart failure. The assumption that all the organs in the body fail in concert is simply not true. There are many older adults who are alert and showing few signs of diminished intellectual capacity, but have a failing heart or damaged liver. People have different rates of organ decline.

In reality, chronological age may tell us very little about the health of an older adult. Rather, functional age, what an older adult can do, is an important indicator of the health status of the older population. Knowing about older people's chronological age is informative (e.g., when someone can apply for Social Security benefits or Medicare), but in order to plan meaningful and effective ministry by, with, and for older adults, we need to know more than just their chronological age. We need to know how their health conditions affect their lives. Their health conditions may very well impact their emotional, psychological, social, and spiritual well-being.

Why do we grow old and what happens to health as we grow older? There are many theories about why we age or grow old. Some scientists believe that our bodies are programmed to age. This means that aging follows a biological timetable, possibly a continuation of the same timetable that controls childhood growth and development. Another group of scientists believe that aging is due to damage to our body systems causing things to go wrong. Two different passages in Scripture speak of the length of human life:

1. "Then the Lord said, 'My spirit shall not abide in mortals forever, for they are flesh; their days shall be one hundred twenty years'." (Genesis 6:3)
2. "The days of our life are seventy years, or perhaps eighty, if we are strong; even then their span is only toil and trouble; they are soon gone, and we fly away." (Psalm 90:10)

Would you like to live to be 120 years old?_____

Why or Why Not? _____

_____

_____

_____

_____

Just as researchers do not agree about why we age, they are not in agreement about when we age. Does aging begin when we are born or when the body has reached maturity?

How do you view aging? Does it begin when you are born? Or, after "mid-life"? Or, once you develop multiple chronic illnesses, such as arthritis, high blood pressure, heart disease, diabetes, and impaired vision and/or hearing? Take time to reflect on your view of when aging really begins

_____

_____

_____

_____

Two terms, Life Expectancy and Life Span, are used interchangeably, but they mean different things. Life expectancy refers to the length of time that one can expect to live. This is calculated by tracking the number of births and deaths that occur each year, along with how old each person was at death. A person born in 1900 could expect to live to age 47. But by 1950, life expectancy had risen to 68 years. Life expectancy today is about 78 years. Of course, with the advancement of age, additional years are projected. For example, a 65-year-old woman today has a life expectancy of about 19 years.

Life Span is the maximum length of life biologically possible for a given species. In humans this is believed to be about 100 to 120 years. Perhaps you have read news reports of people living as long as 122 years. At present time, that would seem to be about the maximum span of time humans can live.

There's no doubt that living longer is the result of advances in medicine and medical procedures. From vaccinations to early diagnosis and long-term treatment, doctors are able to help people fight diseases that were once considered life-threatening. However, we can not ignore the important roles of genetics, environment, and lifestyle. All three are important in determining whether someone will lead a long and healthy life.

Today's older adults are, as a group, healthier and less limited by disabilities than previous generations. Many older adults are becoming increasingly health conscious and taking more responsibility for their physical well-being.

Fitness and Healthy Lifestyles

Perhaps you have heard the expression, "Use it or lose it." In many ways, this is a truism as we age. Good nutrition, exercise, and healthy lifestyles are important to longevity and prevention of chronic illnesses such as osteoporosis, diabetes, and heart disease. Lifestyle choices are extremely important in determining the aging process. Diet, exercise, weight control, vitamin and dietary supplements, stress management and a sense of meaning and purpose are among the top factors that can greatly impact the aging process.

Older adults seeking overall good health and increased longevity need to address the following important components:

- Physical fitness, including strength training and aerobic conditioning
- Proper diet and nutrition
- No smoking
- Regular medical check-ups
- Stress management

Health-related problems can occur as a result of poor nutrition, inactivity, obesity, high cholesterol, failing to control high pressure and other medical disorders, and smoking. By taking an active role in maintaining good health, older adults will be better able to fend off or altogether avoid some of the health-related problems commonly brought on by aging.

How do you rate your health as you are aging? Excellent, Very Good, Good, Fair, or Poor?

_____

Society may view older adults as being frail and in poor health, but older adults themselves don't agree. Several studies indicate that the majority of people 65 years of age and older rate their health as good, very good, or excellent. One study by NCOA, indicates that more than 70% of older adults consider their health to be good or better.

There have been several studies over the years related to health, religion, and aging. Recent research in religious involvement and the overall health of older adults by Harold Koenig and Douglas Lawson found that older adults who have religious involvement have:

- better physical health;
- reduced need for health services (including hospital stays);
- greater sense of well-being;
- experience less depression;
- cope better with stress;
- increased contact with social support networks;
- greater concern for others.

Their study indicates that older adults experience healthier aging as a result of their regular religious involvement. (*Faith in the Future: Healthcare, Aging and the Role of Religion* by Harold G. Koenig, M.D. and Douglas M. Lawson, Ph.D. [Templeton Foundation Press, 2004] p. 10-11)

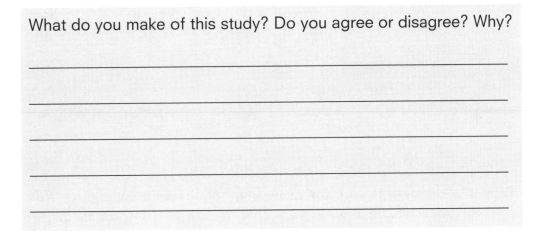

What do you make of this study? Do you agree or disagree? Why?

Chronic Conditions

Unfortunately, chronic conditions are a significant factor for many older adults. As medicine has increasingly controlled infectious disease and acute illnesses (e.g., tuberculosis), chronic disease has become the most prevalent health problem for older adults.

While many older adults continue to lead active and productive lives even with chronic conditions, they generally notice a progression of severity as they get older.

These conditions may have an impact on their spiritual well-being. For example, attending worship services may lessen as a result of difficulty in reading the words in the hymnal or the liturgy in the bulletin, or hearing the speakers at the lectern or pulpit.

Understanding and supporting older adults requires a familiarity with the most common chronic illnesses they face. Keep in mind that chronic conditions are health problems that last for an extended period of time and have no known cure. Chronic conditions are the most prevalent health problems older adults may experience.

Some of the most common chronic illnesses faced by older adults include heart disease, stroke, arthritis, diabetes, cancer, and disorders such as hearing and visual impairments.

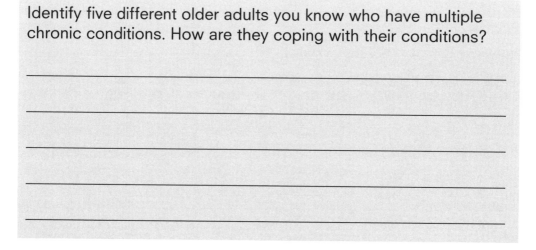

Identify five different older adults you know who have multiple chronic conditions. How are they coping with their conditions?

Pain is a common feature for many older adults who suffer from various chronic conditions. Numerous articles have indicated that pain is frequently undertreated by medical professionals. As a result, depression, social isolation, sleep deprivation, and decreased mobility are all adverse results for older adults who are inadequately treated for chronic pain.

Often older adults will find that their physician, whom they relied on for years, is more attuned to the problems and treatments affecting younger populations and is less knowledgeable concerning the affects of aging. If health problems are not being resolved by their physician or internist, older adults may want to consult a geriatrician.

Geriatricians are medical doctors (MDs) or osteopaths (DOs) who specialize in the diseases and their treatments associated with aging. They have expertise in geriatrics, the medical study of aging. Geriatricians know about the aging process, the impact of aging on illness patterns, drug therapy, health maintenance, and rehabilitation. Unfortunately, there are too few geriatricians in our society and older adults may not live in areas where geriatricians are in practice.

Other helping professions include geriatric nurse practitioners (GNP) and geriatric care managers (GCM). Geriatric nurse practitioners work with physicians and have specialized training in the health and disease issues faced by older adults. Geriatric care managers help older adults stay in their homes and coordinate care services.

Are you aware of any geriatricians, geriatric nurse practitioners, and geriatric care managers in your community?

_____

If not, how can you find out if any such professionals are practicing in your area?

_____

_____

Chronic illness has a dramatic effect on older adults. It significantly reduces their quality of life and decreases their ability to remain independent in their homes. The Centers for Disease Control has indicated that in most cases disability can be delayed as much as ten years by practicing three basic health habits: engaging in regular physical activity, not smoking, and practicing good nutrition. Since poor health and chronic conditions are not inevitable as people age, healthy behaviors can be major factors in how older adults live out their lives in service to God and their neighbors.

Cognitive Aging

Many people believe that dementia is an inevitable part of growing older. Dementia is a pervasive deterioration of intellectual ability that occurs over an extended period of time. But it simply is not true that dementia is a normal part of aging. The reality is that a very small percentage of older adults develop debilitating cognitive disorders.

While dementia is not a normal part of aging, some cognitive changes do occur as people age. Perhaps the most common cognitive change is a decline in speed of mental processing. This is the speed with which older adults are able to take in and process information as they age. For example, in a Bible study class, it may take an older adult a little longer to process new information related to a particular scriptural text compared to a younger person in the class.

Memory loss is the symptom most common in dementia. However, confusion, disorientation, and loss of ability to care for oneself are additional symptoms of cognitive impairment. Perhaps the most common cause of severe cognitive impairment is Alzheimer's disease.

Alzheimer's disease is an irreversible, progressive disease in which the brain undergoes specific changes. With Alzheimer's disease memory loss appears gradually and gets progressively worse over time. The neurons that transmit information in the brain become tangled and coated in plaque so that information is not accurately processed. Keep in mind, however, that just because an older adult is forgetful does not mean that he or she has Alzheimer's disease. In fact, the cause of the problem might be side effects of medications, the most common form of reversible dementia.

If an older adult does have Alzheimer's disease, symptoms of Alzheimer's may progress through three stages. In the early stage of Alzheimer's people begin experiencing short-term memory deficits, difficulty in decision-making, problems in performing routine tasks, personality change and mood changes. Symptoms of early-stage Alzheimer's disease generally present themselves over a two- to four-year period.

During the middle-stage of Alzheimer's disease, memory loss often worsens, communication skills weaken, reasoning becomes difficult, and attention to personal care needs may diminish. This stage can last from two to ten years or more.

In late-stage Alzheimer's disease there is a further decrease in mental function and communication skills. During this stage, people with Alzheimer's disease lose the ability to recognize family members and friends, they cease to speak and eat, lose muscle control and swallow reflexes, slip into a coma, and eventually die. This stage lasts from a few months to three years. But keep in mind, no two people experience Alzheimer's Disease in the same way or at the same rate of progression.

Presently, there is no treatment that can reverse or cure the effects of Alzheimer's disease. However, pharmaceutical research in recent years has led to the development of several medications that, if prescribed early in the disease process, may help to control symptoms and delay the progression of the illness.

According to the Alzheimer Association, 5 million people have the disease today and if no cure is found, as many as 11 to 16 million people may have the disease by 2050. Yet there are steps one can take to reducing the risks of Alzheimer's disease and other forms of dementia:

Eat wisely

Stay physically active

Keep mentally active

Remain socially involved

Do you know someone with Alzheimer's disease? _____

If so, how are they living with the disease?

_____

_____

_____

Depression and Aging

Later life presents older adults with a many challenges. Most older adults have the personal, social, and spiritual resources to understand and deal with these challenges; however, some older adults develop depression. Depression is not a normal part of aging.

With depression, older adults may experience the following symptoms:

- Sleep disturbance
- Loss of interest in pleasurable activities
- Poor attention/concentration
- Loss of appetite
- Agitation
- Irritability
- Memory impairment
- Loss of energy
- Feelings of guilt or regret
- Thoughts of suicide

Depression is treatable and should not be ignored. The incidence of completed suicide is higher among older adults, especially Caucasian men over the age of 74, than for any other age group. While we don't want to negate the needs of older women, particularly since they live longer than men and outnumber older men, the high rate of suicide by older men should cause some alarm. In many of our congregations, women outnumber men in both membership and participation; as a result ministry with older men may be overlooked or worse, undervalued.

What ministries does your church have that meet the needs of older men?

_____

_____

_____

_____

Anti-Aging

As stated earlier, there are few medical professionals with expertise in geriatrics. The career field of geriatrics does not seem to attract physicians as a specialty. This could be a result of geriatric medicine not being valued, our cultural view of aging, inadequate reimbursement, scarcity of academic faculty in geriatrics, or a variety of other barriers to this profession. However, one aging field that appears to be growing is the Anti-Aging Industry—those who offer products and services touted to forestall or reverse aging.

The Bible states, "Vanity of vanities, all is vanity." (Ecclesiastics 1:2) Thousands of years before the manufacture of facial creams, skin tucks, hair restoration, and liposuction, the Old Testament made an observation about the human struggle against vanity. In our society today, adults of every age are increasingly interested in looking and feeling younger and helping them do that is the multi-billion dollar a year anti-aging industry.

While there are no hard statistics on the size of the overall anti-aging movement, industry estimates suggest that it is robust. From eyelid surgery, facelifts, and BOTOX® injections to anti-wrinkle creams, anti-oxidants, and vitamins are all part of the human struggle against time and age. But as one medical doctor concluded, "No matter how clever, how attractive, how entrepreneurial the proponents of anti-aging may be, every one of them will, in time, grow old." (*What are Old People For?* by William H. Thomas, M.D. [VanderWyk & Burnham, 2004]).

How are you facing your own aging? Have you purchased products to keep you looking young? _____

If so, what are they? _____

_____

_____

_____

Have you purchased products to make you feel younger?_____

If so, what are they?

_____

_____

_____

In conclusion, remember what your mother told you, "Don't abuse your body, eat well, and exercise." It is hard work, and people tend to look for easy answers to staying healthy as they age. But older adults will reap considerable benefits. They'll sharply increase their chances of aging well and taking advantage of opportunities to serve God by enjoying the later stages of life.

Retirement and Aging

The Changing Face of Retirement

Retirement is an important topic for leaders in ministry with older adults. Today, people are spending a longer period of time in retirement than ever before. But it is important for us to understand that retirement is a process, not an end in itself. At one time, retirement was thought of as an event. Today, it is more of a process with people moving in and out of retirement. It may mean "bridge" jobs where people prepare for retirement by moving from full-time to part-time work or accept a position which is less stressful or time consuming.

Retirement means for many "freedom from the demands of work." It may mean more control over one's personal time and provide time for new opportunities to learn, give, and grow. But we also need to know that retirement, as an expected part of the lifecycle, came into being only in the 20th century.

Two hundred years ago, people did not retire, at least not in the modern sense of the word. People worked until they "wore out" and died. Usually people died at a much younger age. In fact, life expectancy in 1800 was only 24 years, compared with 77.8 years today. Life was hard. Men often died young as a result of accidents, disease, and from warfare. While for women, a leading cause of death was complications arising from pregnancy and childbirth.

One hundred years ago, people had at best two years of retirement. They worked long and hard and when they could no longer work because of the physical demands of labor, they rested, often in their rocking chairs. During the two years or so of life remaining, people struggled with their failing health and prepared for their impending death. It is this picture of old age that many of us still imagine. Old age is fearful for us in part because we associate growing older with failing health and death.

Today, however, as a result of advances in medicine, scientific discoveries and new technologies, better health and nutrition, job safety, and a host of other variables, people are living longer and healthier than ever before. With more years added to life, people are spending a longer period of time in retirement than ever before. People today can have as much as 20 to 30 years or more in the retirement years.

What would the new retirement age be if most people live to 120?

_____

How long would people stay in school?

_____

How many years would people work?

_____

There is a common stereotype today of retired people sitting in a rocking chair or playing shuffleboard. Actually, as people grow older they are more likely to engage in the same activities that they did before advancing age.

As a result, the concept of retirement is changing in our society. As older adults grapple with a longer life expectancy, an increased need for income security, and a desire to remain engaged professionally, retirement is taking on a new and different meaning.

A new norm of retirement could expand the whole idea of a "second career." Many older adults are working well past the traditional retirement age, returning to the workforce after retirement, or opting for a mix of paid and volunteer work. One "vocational" calling per lifetime may not be adequate fulfillment for most people. The period that we now call "older adulthood" can be redefined not as retirement (i.e., disengagement from meaningful action) but as transition into yet another stage of life's journey.

With so many years of life added beyond the normal retirement age (mid-60s), adults may experience a different kind of retirement in the future. Longer years in retirement may be combined with new opportunities—for second careers, for volunteer roles, for continuing education.

Like Social Security, many laws and attitudes shaping today's retirement options developed around the time of the Great Depression, when high unemployment made it desirable to encourage older Americans to leave the work force.

Times have changed. Now a growing economy may provide opportunities for adults to continue working long past the "normal" retirement age. In addition, there is much speculation that the huge Baby Boom generation (born 1946-1964 and nearing retirement age) will continue to work in retirement (this will be discussed further in Chapter 8). The reasons why Boomers will continue working in retirement are varied but often include: having continuing career interests, wanting to stay productive; changes in type and availability of pension coverage; fearing unstable Social Security and health care coverage; have dwindling retirement investments; and, simply can't afford to retire.

Think for a moment about your own retirement.

Are you retired?_____

Are you planning to retire?_____ When?_____

How do you envision your retirement?
    Continuing to work?
    Going back to school?
    Starting a new career?
    Developing a new business venture?
    Traveling?
    Other ideas?

What about people you know who are retired? Identify someone you know who is retired. How does this person spend his/her days?

_____

_____

What qualities do you admire about this person?

_____

_____

Perhaps an important question for our time is this: Does the institutionalization of retirement perpetuate the ageist myth that older workers can't cut it? In other words, even though many adults might want to work in their retirement years, and may need to do so for financial reasons, keeping or obtaining a job that is both fulfilling and financially rewarding may not be possible. While we may agree that workers should be hired for jobs, and maintain them, because of their job performance, employment is one of the most frequently recognized forms of age discrimination.

Not every older adult who wants to work will be able to do so. Apart from our attitudes about working and our health conditions, searching for a job when we are older becomes harder because of:

- Age discrimination
- Job Obsolescence
- Changing job-performance capabilities
- Employer-sponsored early retirement incentives
- Can you think of other reasons? _____

- _____

As a church leader, you may know older adults who are working or seeking employment. They may be working long past the normal retirement age. It is important to keep in mind that their involvement in ministry may be different from older persons who are fully retired.

Phases of Retirement

Retirement has three distinct phases or stages: Active Phase, Passive Phase, and Final Phase.

Active Phase: During this phase called the "Go-Go" phase, older adults pursue a variety of interests. Some will continue working part-time in the same or similar occupation, while others may return to school, start a new career or business, volunteer, travel, and/or engage in leisure activities. Although there may be some decline in energy and physical functioning and multiple chronic illnesses may occur, older adults in this phase are generally healthy and active. This period of retirement may be short or last years, depending largely upon their health or the health of a spouse, and on financial resources.

Identify persons in your congregation who are in the Active or "Go-Go" Phase of retirement. What are they doing? How are they living as Christian disciples?

_____

_____

_____

_____

Sometimes people will take a short breather from all their activity. After years of working and then doing many things they longed to do, people apparently welcome a period of taking it easy. But after sufficient rest and relaxation, people often become restless and want to re-engage in life. It is at this point that the church can experience some of the greatest growth in disciple-making and service. Older adults may want to reach out in new ways and experience new opportunities for meaningful service.

Identify persons in your congregation who "rested" after retirement and are now involved in a particular ministry. What are they doing? How is their attitude?

_____

_____

_____

_____

Passive Phase: During this phase called the "Slow-Go" phase, energy and health begin to ebb. Extensive travel is replaced with shorter visits to family and friends. An active lifestyle is replaced with a more passive one. Creativity may continue to grow in new ways; however, physical activity lessens and health problems intensify.

Identify persons in your congregation who were once active in the church but who have recently "backed off" from assuming new leadership roles. How are they coping with this change in their lifestyle?

_____

_____

_____

How is your church adapting to these changes in leadership roles?

_____

_____

_____

Sometimes older adults move into the passive phase not because of their own failing health, but because of the health conditions of a spouse or other loved one. Older adults may become heavily involved in a caregiving role (see Chapter 5 for a fuller exploration of this topic) and find that their new lifestyle causes inactivity with the "outside" world. They may be healthy, but their caregiving concerns prevent them from being active and engaged. For many caregivers, their own health over time may deteriorate to the point that once they are no longer responsible for caregiving, they no longer have the energy or health to be active.

Identify caregivers in your congregation who have good health but because of their caregiving responsibilities cannot be more fully involved in the life of the church.

What are ways your congregation is ministering to these older adults?

_____

_____

_____

Final Phase: During this phase called the "No-Go" phase, health problems severely limit or even eliminate most activities outside the home. Mobility is restricted and home health care services or alternative housing may be sought. This phase is defined more by physical and mental changes rather than social changes that accompany the previous two phases.

During the final phase, old age is characterized by extreme physical frailty and disabling chronic conditions are more common. Mental processes slow down and chronic brain conditions (e.g., Alzheimer's Disease) increase with this population of older adults. People in this last phase may feel that death is near.

Identify older persons in your congregation who are in the final phase. Have they talked about death? What are their thoughts?

_____

_____

_____

_____

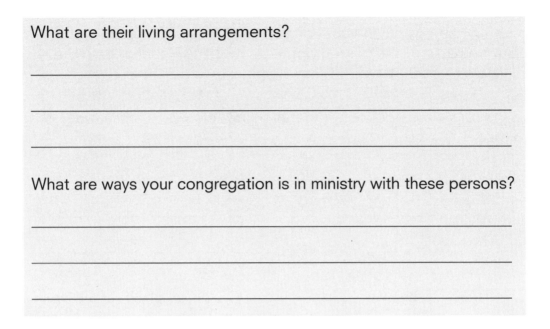

What are their living arrangements?

What are ways your congregation is in ministry with these persons?

Applying chronological ages to any of these phases is not helpful. For example, sometimes we have identified people age 65-74 in the Active Phase, people 75-84 in the Passive Phase, and people 85+ in the Final Phase. This is creating stereotypes and does not necessarily reflect reality. We probably all know someone 85 years of age who has more energy and enthusiasm for life than some people in their 60s. And, we may know people in their early 70s who have multiple chronic conditions that severely limit their mobility and life activity. Chronological age is not always a good determinant of people's ability and health conditions.

Identify an older adult in your congregation who surprises you with their ability and activity for their age. What is it about this person that surprises you?

In addition, there is a common perception of retirement as a perpetual vacation, but it doesn't work that way. After a while, most people become restless and frustrated. Since much of our identity is related to what we do for a living, when we stop working we may feel that life has passed us by, that our life is empty, that we no longer have meaning or purpose. Work provides three important things: *structure* (when you get up in the morning, where you go, how long you stay, and when you come home); *community* (social interaction); and *purpose* (goals and direction). When an older adult retires, they need to replace these three important elements.

In his book, *Aging Well* (Little, Brown and Company, 2002, page 224), Dr. George Vaillant identifies four basic activities that can lead to a rewarding retirement. These four are:

- Develop new social networks to replace co-workers
- Rediscover how to play
- Be creative
- Continue lifelong learning

> Can you identify other activities that might lead to a rewarding retirement? What are they?
>
> _____
>
> _____
>
> _____

As we have seen, the transition from the work force to retirement is often measured in financial and career-centric terms: When is the time right? How big is the nest egg? How to spend it? But often overlooked in that transition are emotional challenges like a change in identity and questions around self-worth and purpose, which can undermine the "golden" years. Often retirees who adjust the best don't think of the transition as retirement because the word carries a passive and negative connotation. Many older adults view the transition as their next career, the next stage, or the next chapter in their life.

Managing Retirement

The process of retirement can be described as having both Push and Pull Factors. Push Factors (e.g., poor health, family caregiving demands), may, in a negative fashion, increase the odds of retirement, sometimes involuntarily. Pull Factors (e.g., travel and leisure plans) may be more positive factors in movement toward retirement

For many older adults, the retirement years can be rewarding. These years provide them with new opportunities to learn, serve, and grow. Older adults can invest themselves in new ways by developing a deepening relationship to God; to their spouse, children, grandchildren, and/or friends; to their community and environment; and, to their own growth and spiritual maturity.

Unfortunately for some older adults, retirement is difficult. Retirement for these folks does not provide an opportunity for joy, pleasure, or fulfillment; rather, it is a time of great distress. Some people worry about becoming ill, losing their memory, being a burden to their family, or outliving their money. People who are more likely to have difficulty include older adults who have:

- Few alternatives
- Little money
- Poor health
- Been over-involved in their work
- Experienced other role losses (e.g., the death of a spouse)
- Can you think of any others? _____
- _____
- _____

What role can the church play in people's lives who are experiencing difficulty in retirement?

_____

_____

Successful retirement includes:

- Careful planning
- Secure financial base
- Good health
- Life purpose
- Growing faith
- Positive attitude

What are ways your church can assist adults and older adults in experiencing successful retirement?

_____

_____

Our society places great emphasis on the productivity of people. Work and employment have become synonymous with meaning and worth. As a result, adjusting to retirement and loss of power can be difficult for older adults. Many older adults will continue to work simply because it is where they find a sense of purpose and control.

Identify older adults you know who have difficulty of "letting go" of control and/or power and of letting God reign supreme in their lives. What are ways they are seeking to maintain power or control?

_____

_____

_____

The church can play an important role in helping older persons come to a new understanding of worth and meaning in life after retirement. Our meaning and worth are not based on work or productivity. It is not based on "who" we are but rather "whose" we are as children created in the image of God. As leaders we may need to help older persons confront not only the physical, financial, and social limitations of old age, but also the vocational limitations, too.

Older adults need to know that there is life after retirement; they need to experience a sense of joy and forgiveness, a sense of peace and justice; they need to know the unconditional love of God.

Mentoring

Retired individuals have opportunities to use the skills and experience they've developed over the years to serve their congregations and communities. Intergenerational connections are important to maintain and to develop as people age and they provide older adults with opportunities to serve as mentors to young people. Whether sharing one's faith with a new Christian or helping a young person in business or career goals, mentors provide guidance, wisdom, knowledge and support in a manner in which a protégé can receive it and benefit from it.

A mentor is different from a tutor. A tutor specializes in content area support. Retired individuals can serve as tutors for children and youth who have questions or difficulty with a class subject such as history, math, science, and English. A mentor, however, develops a relationship with the protégé that provides overall guidance in a field of study or career.

The use of mentor/protégé relationships can be one of the most effective strategies the church can use in attracting, retaining, and making disciples. In this manner, mentoring is a supportive relationship between a mature Christian who shares his/her faith experience, knowledge, and wisdom with another individual who is willing and ready to benefit from this exchange.

Some elements that make for good mentors are:

- Mature Christians
- Good communicators
- Practitioners of the Means of Grace as identified by John Wesley
  - First, do no harm
  - Second, perform acts of mercy
  - Third, observe the ordinances of God
    - Participate in: public worship, study of the Scriptures, Christian conferencing, fasting, and the Lord's Supper
- Genuine love for God and others
- Knowledgeable about the church and community

- Able to apply theory to practice
- Well organized
- Manages time well
- Sense of humor
- Willing to be a mentor, to help guide another

Can you identify someone who was a mentor in your life? Who was this person? What were the qualities that made this person a good mentor?

_____

_____

_____

_____

Can you identify other elements needed for older adults to serve as mentors? What are they?

_____

_____

_____

In developing a mentor/protégé relationship, care must be taken to establish a solid foundation to the relationship. Individual styles differ and need to be respected. The following suggestions can be helpful in establishing a caring, faith-filled relationship:

- Get acquainted: if serving as a faith mentor, share your faith journey
- Discuss what you can offer: information, skills, experience, and wisdom
- Engage in active listening with the protégé
- Discuss what the protégé expects in the relationship
- Discuss your expectations and concerns, if any

- Discuss confidentiality; and, do not break confidence
- Agree on how much time you will spend together for each meeting
- Set a time and place for your next meeting

Can you identify additional guidelines on how to approach developing a mentor/protégé relationship?

_____

_____

_____

_____

Mutual trust, respect and "chemistry" between mentor and protégé are critical to a successful relationship. Sometimes the relationship "clicks" but most often, it develops over time, through effort, prayer, and commitment.

Spirituality and Aging

Finding Meaning in the Later Years

How old would you be if you didn't know how old you are? Do you feel young in some areas of life, but old in others? Do you see yourself as at least ten to fifteen years younger than your chronological age? Or, ten to fifteen years older? While we must accept the reality of growing older, and recognize that aging is part of God's creation, we do not have to live according to the old expectations of chronological age.

Aging is changing. More people are living longer and healthier today than ever before. In many ways a 70-year-old today is more like a 50-year-old twenty years ago.

In the past, when people thought about growing older, they were more influenced by negative stereotypes of aging and focused on disease and disability of older adults. This contributed to our negative views of aging and a denial of it. In denying aging, people didn't prepare for it. But with the changing image of what is possible as we age, we have a growing sense that we can and should do something to help make our aging better.

To age well is to see and know that all of life—at every age and stage—is a gift from a loving, creator God. To live well is to stand against the cultural prejudice about growing old. Affirmation of a person's worth is found in one's "being" not through "having" or "doing." Our worth is not in our ability to be rich, smart, or productive. It is not important "who" we are, but more importantly, "whose" we are. As children of God, we are created in God's own image. If our worth is in what we own or have amassed or the work we have done, in time we will have neither wealth nor possessions. But as children of God, we are and always will be valued, accepted, and loved by God. That's why God sent his Son into the world. God demonstrated his love for us on the cross. The reality is that in spite of ourselves, in spite of our sinfulness and failings, God loves us. As a result, we have a new meaning for our aging. To age well means to creatively accept the many changes in our lives and to maintain a spirit that grows healthier, wiser, and closer to God.

Older adults have the opportunity to redefine the meaning and purpose of their later years. In old age, most adults are not consumed with the demands of work and raising a family. For many people the early years were spent trying to attain some kind of "success," measured differently perhaps for everyone. For some, success was "climbing the ladder" in one's occupation and achieving the top spot. Success was owning a home in the "right" neighborhood, earning a college degree, raising children, or enjoying a long, satisfying relationship with one's spouse. But for many people, the years of adulthood were about attaining and acquiring, about achieving, about success.

How do you measure "success"?

_____

_____

Identify older adults in your congregation who you consider to be successful. What qualities make them successful?

_____

_____

As we grow older, we begin to look at life differently. No longer are we consumed by attaining success. No longer are we driven to achieve. Our values begin to change. Instead of seeking success, instead of competing and being "egocentric," we begin an inward journey. Some people will achieve their goals, realize their dreams, and still find them wanting. Something is missing in their life. For others, they come to the realization that their dreams will never be reached. They can either keep on struggling, trying to succeed, trying to achieve, or something else can happen. It is at this point in life when we move from a living a life based on achieving or acquiring success to living a life based on finding meaning and spiritual maturity.

The Bible is filled with wonderful stories and references relating to the blessings of aging. In Scripture, a long life is often viewed as a reward to the righteous (Psalm 92:12, 14) and sure sign of God's favor (Proverbs 16:31).

In Genesis 12, we read about the call of Abraham. When God first calls Abraham he is getting on in years. In fact, the Bible reports that Abraham is 75 years of age and his wife, Sarah, is advanced in years, too. Interesting that God starts with a late life couple. Why doesn't God start with a young couple? A young couple might have muscles and beauty and an adventurous spirit. Abraham and Sarah are not young. Some might even say that they are old. Yet, God tells them to go forth that they might be a light for all the nations. God calls them into a new life of faith and spiritual insight.

Do you believe that God can use older adults for his purpose? How?

_____

_____

_____

_____

Abraham and Sarah are not running away from persecution. They are not poor. They have a homeland and people who care about them. But something is missing in their life. They are seeking something. And, with God's help, they begin a new journey—to a promised land. Even in their advanced age, their life takes on new meaning and greater purpose.

Identify older adults in your congregation who, in their later years, experienced a new call or vision from God.

_____

_____

_____

In later life, many older adults discover that they can no longer remain in their own homes due to failing health conditions and/or the cost of home maintenance and repair. Sometimes they find it necessary to move into assisted living or nursing home settings. For others, moving into an apartment or with adult children may be their only solution. Such a change can have a dramatic impact on their well-being.

What does this story of Abraham and Sarah say to older adults who no longer can remain in their own homes?

_____

_____

_____

In Exodus 7:7, we read that Moses was 80 years of age when God called him in the form of "a burning bush that was not consumed" to lead God's people out of bondage and slavery in Egypt. Moses, at first, is reluctant to take on such a new venture. He provides God with many reasons why he should not go; but finally, Moses, along with his brother, Aaron, who is 83, make the journey. Let's imagine: Suppose the Israelites who were being held in captivity had seen these two old men walking down a dusty road toward Egypt and had said, "No thank you, God, we'll wait for a younger man or a younger woman to come along." The Israelites still might be held in captivity to this very day! Sometimes we believe that only younger people can be creative in ministry or effective in the service to God. But obviously God does not believe this. God calls and uses people of all ages, including older adults, to fulfill God's will and purposes.

Have you every heard people in your congregation expressing the desire that the Bishop send a younger man or woman to be your pastor? If so, what do you believe? Do you think that only a younger man or woman can be effective in ministry?

_____

_____

_____

God's purposes will not be thwarted, even by advanced age. For example, late in life God blesses with children Abraham and Sarah (Genesis 21:2) and Zechariah and Elizabeth (Luke 1:18, 36). Abraham was perplexed and Sarah laughed upon hearing the news that she would conceive and give birth to a son. To both, such news seemed impossible because of Sarah's old age (Genesis 18). And, in the Gospel of Luke, we read not once but twice (Luke 1:7, 18) that Zechariah and Elizabeth were old—very old. But God uses Elizabeth, who is old enough to know and to understand, to explain to young Mary, mother of Jesus, what was happening in her own life. Elizabeth uses her advantage of age to mentor Mary.

The Scripture is quite clear: God does not stop inviting people into ministry when they reach older adulthood. Nor does God take away God's blessing when people reach 65. The writer of Psalms reminds us, "The righteous flourish like the palm tree, and grow like a cedar in Lebanon . . . In old age they still produce fruit; they are always green and full of sap" (Psalm 92:12, 14). God moves mightily during old age by granting wisdom and other blessings to those who are old, as we read in Job: "Is wisdom with the aged and understanding in length of days?" (Job 12:12).

Identify an older adult in your congregation who has a creative vision for the church. What would he or she like to see happen in your church?

_____

_____

_____

Older adults are invited to make a difference. No longer is there the need "to climb a real or imagined ladder of success." In the later years, most adults have come to realize that their dream is not going to happen. Or, if it has, they are looking for something more fulfilling in life. Older adults can face the loss of sight, hearing, mobility or even money, but the loss of meaning or purpose may be the most painful.

It is at this time in our lives that we have an opportunity to move beyond success to a higher quality of spiritual maturity. Older adults are invited by God to seek a life of meaning and purpose even in advanced age.

In order for older adults to make a difference in the world, older adults must focus on adding life to one's years, not just adding years to one's life. It is more important to look for the "Fountain of the Living Well" rather than the "Fountain of Youth." In accepting the fact of aging and the reality of death, older adults must:

- Be ready to make difficult choices. Which values are still important? Do I really need that big house after all these years? Do I really need to spend so much time "perfecting" my golf game? Can I lead a fulfilling life as a widow or widower? How can I make a difference in my church or community?
- Remain open to change. We can't keep adding new projects, new responsibilities or new values without getting rid of some old ones. Each stage of life calls for the substitution of new skills, activities, and relationships for old ones that are no longer important in our life. What is God calling me to be? What is most important in my life at this time? What do I need to stop doing in order to make a difference in the world today?
- Be open to new roles and responsibilities. As older adults, we can assume new roles as teachers or mentors—encouragers and supporters of others. We are no longer interested in just attending meetings and generating ideas; we also want to see our ideas carried out. We know that if we want to make a difference in the world, we must stop dreaming about it and get started.

Aging Successfully?

One day, many years ago while serving as a pastor of a church in Pennsylvania, I visited my friend Jennie. At 87 years of age, Jennie was still quite active and involved in her church and community. In addition to serving on church committees, participating in community functions, and transporting her friends by car to various activities, Jennie taught a women's Sunday school class—something she had been doing for nearly 70 years. During my visit with Jennie I told her that I was moving to Nashville, Tennessee to work for one of our denominational agencies as the director of older adult ministries. I shared with her my feelings about being called by God into the field of religious gerontology and of my passion for wanting to help congregations in their ministry with older adults. Although my leaving was a great disappointment to her, especially after she realized that I would no longer be her pastor, she said, "Well, now someone can tell me how to grow old!"

In the marketplace today there are many books available that purport to help adults learn what it means to age "successfully." At least two authors suggest that "successful aging" means: avoidance of disease and disability, maintenance of cognitive and physical function, and sustained engagement with life (*Successful Aging* by John Rowe and Robert Kahn [New York: Random House, 1998]).

We can add some additional components related to our own understanding and beliefs about "successful aging."

- *Health.* "If you have your health," so the old adage goes, "you have everything!"
- *Income.* Having a secure financial base is important for our later years. Many older adults worry about their financial future the longer they live.
- *Keeping Busy.* Rather than traditional measures of health or money, some people believe that simply "keeping busy" is important for successful aging.
- *Attitude.* Likewise, optimism and effective coping styles (attitudes) may be an important key to successful aging.

These suggestions are valuable and can be tremendously helpful if one is talking about "successful aging." But I wonder, in the Judeo-Christian tradition, are we necessarily talking about "successful" aging? Or, do we mean something different . . . something even more significant?

Of course, no one really sets out to "fail" in aging. We are part of a society that promotes "success" over "failure." And, for many young and middle aged adults, aging and growing older doesn't seem so "successful" an achievement in life. Indeed, we live in an age-denying, age-defying culture. Such thinking is often influenced by negative stereotypes of aging and focused on disease and disability of older adults. This attitude contributes to our negative views of aging and a denial of it. In denying aging, people don't prepare for it. But this isn't the whole story: aging is changing. Or at least the people who are growing older are.

The fact that so many people are living longer and healthier today is a reality that we cannot ignore. We have moved from a time not long ago when aging was seen as synonymous with senility and death, to one in which a glimpse of human potential has opened up incredible possibilities. Surely, God must have some purpose for adding years to our lives.

As people are living longer and healthier lives, I believe faith communities are called to provide a different understanding of aging. Faith communities should be less concerned about helping people age "successfully" but rather, helping people age "faithfully." An important role for the church in ministry with older adults is precisely this: helping older adults age in faith. In other words, inviting, nurturing and equipping older adults for spiritual growth and maturity.

Unfortunately, effective congregational ministries that focus on the life experiences and spiritual needs of older adults are often absent. Many churches have not sensed that the elderly have a unique calling; that God invites and uses people at every age and stage of life for the building of the kingdom. Instead, an aging church, with growing numbers of older adults, indicates a fatal situation, measuring significance only in terms of young people.

Breaking through the myths and stereotypes of aging is important for most congregations. Pastors, lay speakers, and other church leaders play an important role in helping the church develop intentional ministry with older adults that encourages and empowers older adults to age faithfully. The faith, wisdom, and experience of older adults should not be ignored simply because of one's age or stage in life. Aging in faith is important for persons at any age, but particularly important for people in the later years.

Recently, I had a conversation with a woman who was a participant in one of my seminars on aging and older adult ministries. She shared with me that following the death of her husband her self-esteem was shattered. She felt confused and had lost a sense of purpose in her life. She didn't feel like doing much but she had been encouraged to participate in my seminar. She felt blessed by what she had heard and experienced. And, as a result of the seminar, she felt God speaking a message of hope for her life.

Following the seminar, she publicly proclaimed to all who had gathered that she felt God wasn't finished with her yet. She was excited and enthusiastic about her life and what God might be leading her to do next. She had come to believe that even in her later years, God still had a purpose for her life. She was grateful to God and appreciative of my leadership in the seminar.

I was grateful for her comments and encouraged by her enthusiasm. Yet as she walked away, I wondered about her local church. Would her congregation encourage her in her faith journey? Would her congregation help her know and experience

God's love through Jesus Christ? Would her congregation provide her with the necessary resources for living her faith in every day life?

Many congregations today are so focused on reaching young people that they may ignore the spiritual needs of older adults. In addition, many church leaders, who may be older themselves, may mistakenly believe that older adults already have a deep and abiding faith. That they don't need further spiritual growth. Or, if they do need to grow in faith, they can do so on their own. As a result, older adults have faith needs that may be overlooked by active, growing congregations. While we are called to make disciples of Jesus Christ, this doesn't mean just making disciples of children, youth, and young adults! Older adults need to experience a new (or renewed) relationship with God through Jesus Christ and to grow in faith maturity, too. As we have witnessed through Scripture, older adults have valid and vital roles needed by their faith communities. Unfortunately, when older adults see little interest directed at them by the church, they gradually lose their sense of themselves as having value and worth. They may begin to believe that their life and faith are not important to God or to the church.

Aging Faithfully

As people age, their spiritual maturity is tested and refined through the frequent experience of loss, in the form of illness and disability, death of loved ones, and changes in social position and economic conditions. As a result, the aging process adds a new dimension to our understanding of faith. As we grow older our challenges are often greater. So, what does "aging faithfully" mean?

To age faithfully is to see and know that all of life—at every age and stage—is a gift from a loving, creator God. In the Scriptures we read that we have been created in the image of God. We are uniquely made and wonderfully formed by God. But God's love for us doesn't stop when we are born. "Listen to me, O house of Jacob . . . even to your old age I am he; even when you turn gray I will carry you. I have made, and I will bear; I will carry and will save" (Isaiah 46:3, 4). God's love for us never ends. In the midst of losses and the challenges of life, aging faithfully means knowing that all of life is a precious gift of a loving, caring God.

To age faithfully is to trust the promises of God. While the specific nature of the promise may vary, depending upon particular needs and circumstances, the fact remains that God's grace is the source of God's promises. To aging persons, the promise is God's loving presence and strength. To the suffering, the promise is God's saving presence and help. To the sick, the promise is healing and comfort.

To the sinner, there is God's promise of forgiveness. To the dying, the promise is eternal life. Therefore, to age faithfully is to see and know that all of life—at every age and stage—is a gift of a loving, creator God. God's gift of long life provides for older adults an opportunity to deepen their relationships with God, who promises to love, forgive, bless, and sustain. With the Psalmist, people aging faithfully are able to sing: "This God—his way is perfect; the promise of the Lord proves true; he is a shield for all who take refuge in him" (Psalm 18:30).

To age faithfully is to stand against the cultural prejudice about growing old. The folly of many older adults is the effort to deny or defy aging, to continue worshiping at the shrine of youth and young adulthood. The multi-billion dollar a year "anti-aging" medical and cosmetic industries keep alive the notion that young is beautiful and old is ugly. As a result, the concept of anti-aging has captured the interest of many older adults. Aging faithfully means refusing to accept this supposition. We need to be reminded that "The glory of youth is their strength, but the beauty of the aged is their gray hair" (Proverbs 20:29). Relaxing our defenses concerning our wrinkles, graying hair, even our sagging tummies, etc., is the path toward spiritual maturity. This does not mean that we don't take proper care of our minds, our bodies, and ourselves. Rather, to age faithfully means to creatively accept the many changes in our lives and to maintain a spirit that grows healthier and wiser.

To age faithfully means that we develop a new understanding of self-worth. Throughout our lives we are taught in countless ways by society that our worth is determined by our productivity. But as mature adults, we are able to affirm the value God placed upon human life, not a worth dependent on the amount or quality of work that a person does. As stated previously, affirmation of a person's worth is found in one's "being," not through "having" or "doing." It is not important "who" we are, but more importantly, "whose" we are. We sing with the Psalmist, "I have been young, and now am old, yet I have not seen the righteous forsaken . . ."(Psalm 37:25).

To age faithfully is to be part of a congregation that knows that spiritual growth is possible and relevant for older adults. To be part of a congregation that invites and equips older adults for experiencing a new or renewed relationship with God. Older adults, no less than persons of all ages, need to grow in faith. "Then afterward I will pour out my spirit on all flesh; your sons and your daughters shall prophesy, your old men shall dream dreams, and your young men shall see visions" (Joel 2:28). Without a growing faith, older adults lack the resource of the One who can give life meaning, purpose and hope in times of fear, loss, and uncertainty.

Finally, to age faithfully means to practice the spiritual disciplines. Praying, reading the Bible, attending and participating in worship, receiving the sacraments of Holy

Baptism and Holy Communion, sharing the experiences of faith with others, and meeting the needs of others are just some of the many ways older adult can know and experience faithful aging. As we age faithfully we are invited to hear and respond to the words of Micah: "With what shall I come before the LORD, and bow myself before God on high? God has told you, O mortal, what is good; and what does the LORD require of you but to do justice, and to love kindness, and to walk humbly with your God" (Micah 6:6a, 8).

Identify additional resources within your religious tradition that provide the later years with opportunities for aging faithfully.

_____

_____

_____

What are ways your congregational can be intentional in helping older adults age faithfully?

_____

_____

Creating a Spiritual Legacy

As we grow older, we might be considered a generation of "wisdom keepers" who have much wisdom and life experience to hand on to younger generations. We read in the Psalms: "O God, from my youth you have taught me, and I still proclaim your wondrous deeds. So even to old age and gray hairs, O God, do not forsake me, until I proclaim your might to all the generations to come" (Psalm 71:17-18). Like the psalmist, we have a responsibility to share what we have learned from life with our children and grandchildren, with our family, with our friends, and with our church and community.

Perhaps the reason we have increased in life expectancy today compared to a hundred years ago is because the world so desperately needs the wisdom of older adults. God has gifted us with the wisdom of age to pass on to those who will listen.

We need to be persistent because seniors are sometimes not listened to, simply because of their age.

It is important to recognize that as we grow older, we may have more questions than answers. Living a long life and growing in faith, we may come to realize that we do not have all the answers to our many questions about the mysteries of our faith. Other questions might be more about our own life and may include:

- What do I love?
- What do I need to give up and what do I need to hold on to?
- What is unfolding in my life?
- How do I want to be remembered?

In the movie *About Schmidt*, Jack Nicholson portraits Warren Schmidt, a man in his 60's who is forced to deal with an ambiguous future as he enters retirement. He and his wife buy an RV vehicle and have great dreams of traveling across the country. Shortly after retirement his wife dies, and so do his dreams. While trying to run his daughter's life, he realizes that he wasted his. At this point, he proclaims: "Relatively soon, I will die. Maybe in 20 years, maybe tomorrow, it doesn't matter. Once I am dead and everyone who knew me dies too, it will be as though I never existed. What difference has my life made to anyone? None that I can think of. None at all."

How sad for Warren Schmidt. How sad for anyone who believes that his or her life makes no difference. There is an African proverb that goes something like this: "When an old person in the tribe dies, a whole library disappears." We are reminded that wisdom and experience can be lost, if they are not shared.

As in all other stages of personal development, aging encompasses special tasks, specifically the desire to leave a legacy (to be remembered) and the ability to put one's life story into a meaningful whole. People want to leave behind more than just a stock portfolio. They want to leave part of themselves. The legacy of one's ethics, values, and life stories is a focus for many older adults.

Some older adults are great philanthropists. People like Ruth Lilly, Michael Bloomberg, Bill and Melinda Gates, Ted Turner, Martha Ingram, and Cal Turner quickly come to mind as people who are attempting to help mitigate social ills. Of course, there are many others who are not so famously known. People who have amassed sizeable incomes and provide financially for foundations, including the poor, higher education, hospitals, the arts, and medical research. We have many older adults in our congregations who are capable and willing to make generous financial gifts to and through the church. Opportunities for the church to be the benefactor of such generous gifts should never be ignored. Often people desire to give generously in thankfulness to God and for the blessings in their life. In fact, older adults should be invited to explore opportunities for such giving in the church and made aware of how they might make bequests and include the church in their will.

But beyond leaving material possessions and valued treasures, perhaps the greatest lasting legacy for older adults is best reflected in the life they have lived. As people grow older, their perspective about their importance and their ambitions change. Church leaders can help older adults discover what they can offer to others by inviting them to ask the following questions:

What needs do you see in your family?

_____

What needs do you see in your church?

_____

What needs to you see in your community?

_____

Who are some people who could benefit from your wisdom and life experiences?

_____

Additional questions, might include:

How do you want to be remembered?

_____

What are some wise things you have learned over the years?

_____

What does society or your church need to hear from you?

_____

What is one story or event you want to pass on to the next generation?

_____

What personal legacy do you hope remains after you are gone?

_____

What ways can your church help you create a legacy?

_____

You may also want to invite older adults to make a time line of their life journey. This form of life review provides an opportunity for older adults to reminisce. By taking a sheet of paper and drawing a straight line in the middle of the paper, persons are asked to mark the beginning of their life with the year of their birth and the age of their life presently (see Appendix A, Adult Faith Journey). Next, invite older adults to indicate the high points and the low points of their life along the way. Where did they experience God in their life? Where did they experience emptiness in their life? And, so on. Older adults are then able to capture a glimpse of their life in retrospect and help find meaning and fulfillment.

From this new perspective, older adults can be invited to jot down ideas about using their unique gifts in creating a legacy and in making a difference in the lives of those around them. Some idea starters include:

- Record your life story and faith journey: journal, videotape, create a scrapbook
- Mentor youth in the confirmation class and new adult church members
- Volunteer in a nursing home
- Serve in a food shelter
- Telephone persons who are confined to their homes
- Visit people who are lonely
- Become involved in peace and justice issues

Caregiving and Aging

Who are Caregivers?

"When Jesus saw his mother and the disciple whom he loved standing beside her, he said to his mother, 'Woman, here is your son.' Then he said to the disciple, 'Here is your mother.' And from that hour, this disciple took her into his own home" (John 19:26, 27).

Even as Jesus hung on the cross, despite his own agony and pain, he looked down, saw his mother, and had compassion for her. Before he died, Jesus entrusted his mother's care to another disciple. Jesus was concerned about his mother's well-being and, before he died, he made certain his mother was being cared for.

In the Bible, we find older adults very much a part of the family and the community. Older persons, especially the frail and infirm, were cared for by their families. In The Letter of James we read, for example, "Religion that is pure and undefiled before God, the Father, is this: to care for orphans and widows in their distress" (James 1:27).

Former First Lady Rosalyn Carter is credited with saying that "there are four kinds of people in the world . . .

- Those who have been caregivers
- Those who are currently caregivers
- Those who will be caregivers
- Those who will need caregivers"

Older adults struggle not only with the awareness that their time on earth is growing shorter but also with the debilitations occasioned by aging. Many among the elderly need courage and support to keep living. Many older adults will require some form of caregiving or will become caregivers themselves.

Caregiving is often defined as one person giving care to another. It is a process that often involves tremendous sacrifice of time, energy, and money. It is often emotionally charged and demanding.

Caring for a family member can be very rewarding, but it is also hard work, and caregivers are often filled with conflicting roles and emotions. Caregiving often means sacrificing one's own pastimes and plans for the good of someone else. Older adults, especially women, who provide long-term care for a chronically ill loved one, can experience physical and health problems and often suffer serious long-term financial consequences—including reduced Social Security, pension, and retirement income—as a result of reduced time in the workforce.

Who are the caregivers? There are approximately 45 million caregivers in the United States (21% of the adult population), according to a new study conducted for the National Alliance for Caregiving and AARP and funded by the MetLife Foundation (for more info, go to www.aarp.org/research). The study found that caregivers are desperate for support, including direct assistance as well as information.

In addition, a new Fact Sheet developed by the National Center on Caregiving at Family Caregiver Alliance describes some important issues related to caregiving (690 Market St., Ste 600, San Francisco, CA 94104. Phone: 415-434-3388 or 1-800-445-8106. Email: info@caregiver.org. Website: www.caregiver.org).

- The average caregiver is a 46-year-old married woman who works outside the home earning an annual income of $35,000
- The value of informal caregiving provided by women in the United States is in the range of $148-$188 billion annually.
- Women are likely to spend a total average of 12 years out of the workforce raising children and caring for an older relative or friend.

- Although men also provide assistance (and about 39% of caregivers are men), female caregivers may spend as much as 50% more time providing care than male caregivers.
- 33% of working women decreased their work hours to care for a chronically ill loved one; 29% passed up a job promotion, training, or assignment; 16% quit their jobs; and 13% retired early.
- Women who provide care for an ill or disabled spouse are six times as likely to suffer symptoms of depression or anxiety as those who had no caregiving responsibilities.
- 25% of women caregivers report health problems resulting from their caregiving activities.
- The challenges of caregiving also have a positive side, however: Many women caregivers report feeling a stronger sense of purpose in life than their non-caregiving women peers, as well as more autonomy and personal growth.

With decreasing federal and state dollars and with society's challenge to provide effective, quality health care, the church is faced with new and exciting opportunities for helping both care-receivers and caregivers.

Caregiver Support Groups

While we read and hear much about our aging church and society, it is important to remember that most older adults live independently and are active in their families and communities. As mentioned earlier, less than 5% of the older adult population resides in long-term care facilities or nursing homes, and most older persons are never institutionalized on a permanent basis. When older adults become frail or dependent, however, family support networks usually provide caregiving.

As people grow older, they may become less able to perform major roles in adulthood. One common measure of functional ability is the Activities of Daily Living (ADL). ADLs refer to basic personal care activities such as: feeding, toileting, dressing, bathing, and transferring (from bed to chair, for example). While another measure of functional ability is the Instrumental Activities of Daily Living (IADL). IADLs are activities needed for independent living, including using the telephone, preparing meals, shopping, handling finances, and taking medications by oneself. ADLs and IADLs are most often used to identify caregivers, to measure the level and type of work that caregivers perform, and to understand care recipients' needs.

Until recently, the work that family members and friends did to help frail or disabled members of society remained relatively invisible due to a lack of attention. Family members have traditionally been and continue to be the principal source of service and support for functionally dependent older persons, as well as chronically disabled loved ones of any age. Families provide a wide range of assistance, from occasional help with shopping and transportation to financial assistance to primary in-home caregiving. Wives and daughters most often fill the caregiver role, but husbands, sons, and other family members and friends also frequently care for frail or dependent older adults.

This help is not without its price, however. Caregivers can experience weariness and often feel discouraged from the lack of emotional support and the difficulty of finding needed help. Many caregivers are unaware of available resources for assistance. While some caregivers seldom leave the house for relaxation or respite, others are busy juggling family, work, and personal needs. Stress, fatigue, and anger may be experienced by the most loving caregiver.

At any stage of caregiving, especially caregiving that may become more and more of a responsibility as the older adult experiences increasingly declining health, the family member must review the situation and determine whether becoming, or remaining, the primary caregiver for that individual is best for themselves and for the family member.

Identify caregivers in your congregation. What are their needs or concerns?

_____

_____

_____

What are ways your congregation can help to meet these needs?

_____

_____

_____

The church can and should take necessary steps to help family caregivers as they provide support for loved ones. One important approach for churches to take is to establish a caregiver support group. While starting a caregiver support group is just one of many possibilities for congregations to become more intentional in assisting caregivers, this is an important, yet often over looked, ministry.

By participating in a caregiver support group, family members can experience numerous benefits:

- First, the caregiver's feelings of loneliness and isolation are reduced in the non-judgmental company of others facing similar situations.
- Second, the caregiver receives information about the aging process and about available community resources.
- Third, interaction among caregivers with similar problems and concerns helps develop skills in stress management, problem solving, communication, and home care techniques.
- Fourth, group participation builds a support network that may well carry over beyond group meetings into lasting friendships.
- Fifth, and finally, opportunities for the spiritual growth of both the caregiver and the frail or dependent family member can be enhanced.

As a church leader, when starting a caregiver support group, you will want to become knowledgeable about your community resources. Although communities differ in the types and number of resources they offer, certain core services supported by government funding, private funding, or private enterprise are available in most areas. You will want to contact the social services department of your local hospital or other health care facility. Also, many nursing homes and other long-term care facilities have social workers on staff. Social workers and other staff can be helpful in providing important information about the availability of local resources. In addition, you may contact your local Area Agency on Aging office. The staff of this agency knows many of the services already being provided in your community.

Provide respite care services for caregivers. If necessary, receive a "love offering" in your church for persons providing caregiving for loved ones. Since caregivers often have added expenses and reduced incomes, a "love offering" is one way of showing your congregation cares. By creating caregiver support groups in your congregation, you can help primary caregivers provide vital and loving care for frail and dependent older adults or for chronically disabled persons of any age.

Volunteers in Caregiving

The Ten Commandments offer an oft-repeated admonition: "Honor your father and your mother, so that your days may be long in the land that the Lord your God is giving you" (Exodus 20:12). These instructions, although emphasized in many children's Sunday school curriculum, were established as binding upon adults. Adults are to honor their parents. The Jewish law required that children were to provide for the care and welfare of their parents.

In spite of our emphasis on youth and technology, there is a responsibility incumbent upon each generation to provide care for its frail elderly. In our own time, this will prove to be of increasing expense, as the resources necessary to care for an older generation become more costly. But there is something more important than the expense to consider. There is the moral integrity of our society and the mission of the church at stake.

Demographic changes and several trends in our society have increased the risk of becoming a caregiver at some time—or multiple times—during a lifetime.

- Adults can expect their parents and partners to live longer lives, which increases the risk that chronic illnesses and functional disability will occur that will require years of caregiving.
- The decline in overall family size means that caregiving responsibilities for aging parents are falling on fewer shoulders than they did in the past.
- A higher divorce rate is contributing to a larger share of middle-aged and older persons living without a spouse, thereby accelerating the rate at which care from someone outside of the household may be needed
- At the same time, the dramatic increase in the rate of women's paid employment has made it problematic to assume that full-time women homemakers can be counted on to care for the increase in the number of frail elderly.

In addition, caregiving needs have also intensified as efforts to contain health care costs have shortened hospital stays and shifted greater responsibilities outside of hospital walls and into homes.

In their book, *Faith in the Future*, Harold Koenig and Douglas Lawson state that "the true need as our population ages will be for the church to train volunteer caregivers and other volunteers to interact with the growing numbers of older adults." With our increasing older population, the demands for caregiving will grow dramatically. However, with the declining availability of relatives to provide assistance, there will be a significant shrinkage in the supply of informal caregivers. Who will care for such a large population for frail elders, if not the family? The government? Perhaps to some extent, but with increasing costly healthcare, how much will the government provide? A major factor standing in the way of any real reform in governmental policy for caregiving is the fact that much of long-term care has been provided by the family, especially women, on an unpaid basis.

The role of caregiving by congregations will become even more crucial as the older adult population continues to increase in numbers. By the 2030's, for example, a substantial proportion of Baby Boomers (see Chapter 8) will be 80 and older. As a result, the demand for long-term care will grow dramatically.

As congregations consider both the spiritual and physical health of older members, they will want to put in place a Congregational Health Ministry, including a Parish Nurse Ministry. Some of the responsibilities of a Parish Nurse are to coordinate regular health screenings (e.g., high blood pressure, cholesterol levels, diabetes, etc.), serve as health educator and personal health counselor, provide referral and resource information, coordinate caregiving volunteers, develop support groups, and advocate on behalf of the health and welfare of members.

Specific congregational health ministries might include Adult Day Services and Respite Care. The church should provide the use of its facilities for an Adult Day Service, as many might do for child care. Congregations should also train volunteers to visit the care recipients' homes, providing relief for the caregiver.

Congregations wanting to develop intentional caregiving ministries should keep the following priorities in mind:

- Allow care recipients to remain as independent as possible for as long as possible.
- Intervene gracefully and prayerfully and only when necessary.
- Get and give up-to-date information on health issues.
- Don't take on too much responsibility.
- Manage stress.
- Get help when needed.

Caring for an older parent, relative, neighbor, or church member can be joyous and enriching. Caregivers can gain wisdom from care recipients as they tell their stories and share their faith. Through caregiving, individuals are able to practice spiritual habits of service and self-sacrifice.

Does your church have a Congregational Health Ministry or Parish Nurse Ministry? If yes, what are its responsibilities? If no, how would you go about starting such a ministry?

_____

_____

_____

_____

Elder Abuse and Neglect Issues

An all-too-frequent crime against older adults is *Elder Abuse*. As a result of what was discussed earlier (e.g., the growing population of older adults, people living longer and with more chronic conditions, fewer family caregivers, and less government support, etc.) elder abuse may become one of the most frequent yet underreported crimes in society. Sadly, elder abuse is often related to the stresses of caregiving.

There are two categories of elder abuse: Domestic elder abuse and Institutional abuse. Domestic elder abuse is the mistreatment of an older adult by someone who has a special relationship with the elder (spouse, sibling, adult children, friend, or other caregiver). The abuse normally takes place in the older person's home or in the home of the caregiver.

Institutional abuse is the mistreatment of an older adult who lives in a nursing home or other residential setting. Abusers are usually paid staff or other professional caregivers who are supposed to be providing care and protection.

Church leaders and volunteer visitors should be aware of the various types of elder abuse. These are:

- *Neglect* is the failure of a caregiver (or the elderly person, *self-neglect*) to provide goods or services that are necessary for optimal function or to avoid harm.
- *Psychological/Emotional Abuse* is conduct that causes mental anguish in an elderly person.
- *Abandonment* is when the family or caregiver completely abandons the older person—whether in their home or by placing them in an institution.

- *Physical/Sexual Abuse* is an act that may result in pain, injury, impairment or illness. Sexual abuse is any non-consensual sexual contact.
- *Financial Exploitation* is the misappropriation of an older adult's financial assets for the benefit of another. According to the National Center on Elder Abuse there are about 5 million cases of elder exploitation a year.

Older adults are often quite vulnerable to abuse. People who are concerned about having enough income to last them through their lives may be more likely to fall for a scheme that promises to increase their assets and the income from those assets. Older adults may have cognitive problems that make it more difficult for them to understand the consequences of their decisions. They may be lonely or isolated and fear that reporting an abuser will lead to their being without a caregiver. If it is a family member who is the abuser, an older adult may feel like he or she deserves such treatment because of some past issue or incident. Further, abuse by a family member may go unreported because of fear or embarrassment on the part of the older adult.

If you knew an older adult in your church was being abused, how would you handle the situation?

_____

_____

If you knew an older adult in your church was experiencing self-neglect, how would you handle this situation?

_____

_____

One thing is certain, church leaders are not above the law. If you suspect elder abuse, contact your state Adult Protective Services (APS) agency to have them investigate.

In an effort to minimize any potential for elder abuse, caregivers must be attuned to their own needs. Caregivers must recognize what causes stress and establish a plan that will mitigate the stress. Stress reduction takes place physically, emotionally, spiritually, and mentally. Caregivers need to assess how they are doing on a daily basis. It is helpful for caregivers to simplify life as much as possible; to learn about the health issues of the care recipient; to develop caregiving plans; to set boundaries related to time, money, and privacy; and to build supportive networks.

Grandparents Raising Grandchildren

"Over the river and through the woods, to grandmother's house we go." Lyrics written in 1844 by Lydia Maria Child paint a quaint picture of a family making their way to grandmother's house on Christmas Day. But in today's world, that picture doesn't always reflect reality. Many children are already living in a grandparent-headed household. And, for many of these children, no parent is living there—the grandparent is the primary caregiver.

For many people, one of the great joys in life is being a grandparent; but today, increasing numbers of grandparents are raising grandchildren. According to the 2000 United States Census, more than six million children in the United States are living in households headed by grandparents or other relatives. Over a third of these grandparents (2.4 million) are primarily responsible for meeting the basic needs of these children.

Grandparents raising grandchildren are responding to a problem in the middle (parent) generation, such as a death of the parent, illness, divorce, immaturity, teenage pregnancy, incarceration of the parent, military service, parental substance abuse, child abuse, or neglect. Grandparents are motivated by the love they feel for their grandchildren and step in to fill a gap created by the problem.

But the challenges many of these families face can seem insurmountable. Grandparents raising grandchildren must deal with issues relating to child care, education, medical care (including insurance coverage), legal concerns, faith development, and emotional support. In most instances, grandparents simply did not expect to be parents again!

For grandparents, shortages of time and money, declining health, unfamiliarity with existing community resources (especially in the fields of medical care and education), and confusing legal problems often combine to create grief, guilt, and stress. In addition, grandparents may fear that they will become ill, disabled, or die and no one will be available to care for their grandchildren. They see themselves as the last, if not best, hope for their grandchildren.

While grandparent-headed families cross all races and socio-economic levels, these grandparents are more likely to live in poverty than other grandparents. As a result, grandparents may not be able to afford appropriate medical care if their grandchildren become ill or disabled.

Grandparents who may have been planning their retirement now have children in their house who need to get to school, have medical attention, and get to extracurricular activities. In addition, raising grandchildren sometimes isolates grandparents from their peers, often leaving them feeling depressed and lonely.

Grandparents often lack information about the range of support services, benefits and policies they need to fulfill their caregiving role. As a result, grandparents parenting the second time around need social support as well as up-to-date information about effective parenting and available community services.

Churches can play a valuable role in helping grandparents who are raising their grandchildren by;

- Providing educational seminars on parenting
- Starting support groups and respite care for grandparents
- Listening empathically to grandparents
- Providing childcare services for various church activities and functions
- Establishing a volunteer force to help with minor home repair and maintenance
- Gathering and sharing information about community resources
- Encouraging grandparents to avail themselves to community resources
- Praying with and for grandparents and children
- Creating models of intergenerational Bible study
- Taking "love offerings" for grandparents raising grandchildren
- Advocating for grandparents'/grandchildren's rights

What are ways your church can respond in helping to meet the needs of grandparents raising grandchildren?

_____

_____

_____

_____

What are ways your church can respond in helping to meet the needs of children being raised by their grandparents?

_____

_____

_____

_____

Providing information and support for grandparents will benefit both grandparent and grandchildren. Church support of grandparents and grandchildren is an integral part of the faith development of both, and influences their chances for deepening their love for God and for one another.

CHAPTER 6

Death and Aging

Our Cultural Understanding of Death

Growing older is no longer synonymous with death. Older adults are living longer and generally healthier lives today than previous generations of seniors. Yet, paradoxically, it is the older adult who is seen as the primary herald or omen of death. It is no longer a bolt out of the blue that carries off one's children; rather, it is the gradual wasting process that finally provides release for the elderly.

In the early 1900s, death often came at infancy or at a very young age. People died from injuries, childbirth, or a sudden illness that could not be cured. Today, most people live to old age. Medical advances have contributed greatly to the prolongation of life and, as a result, death most often comes later in life. While many older adults would prefer to die at home, the majority of deaths in the United States occur in hospitals or nursing homes. Sustaining life and preventing death for as long as possible is a hallmark of the tremendous advances in medical technology. However, our success at prolonging life has been accompanied by a reluctance to deal with death.

Just as we have come to rely on the medical system to prevent death, we have come to rely on other professionals to deal with death once it occurs. We remove all evidence of death from our sight. The funeral industry has become firmly established in our culture of death, offering products and services, including funeral planning, casket selection, and body preparation. In our culture, death is dealt with in a very prescribed and often impersonal way, with laws and regulations guiding how to handle the body and how to file the necessary paperwork.

Even our expressions of grief and mourning reflect a cultural emphasis on minimizing disruption and getting back to work and everyday routines. Many companies have policies about how long people can stay home from their jobs when there is a death in the family, even specifying what degree of kinship is required before any time off is allowed.

Often our cultural attitude is to remove the remnants of death as quickly as possible and to move on. Even older adults, after experiencing the death of a long-time partner or friend, may quickly be forgotten by their friends and the church. They may mourn alone with feelings of sorrow, anger, guilt, and confusion that can result or arise from the experience of loss.

Next to aging and growing old, the subject of death is perhaps the most significant taboo of our times. Pastors often fail to discuss issues of death and dying with parishioners. Even in the church death is often disguised or camouflaged through euphemistic language. People simply do not say that someone is "dead" or "died"; rather, they say that someone has "been lost" or "passed away." The language we use speaks volumes about our desire to deny or defy death.

There are many reasons why the subject of death is so avoided in our culture. Several of these include the following:

1. Most of us no longer live in rural settings or on farms that subtly but constantly remind us of the natural cycles of birth and death (e.g., planting and harvesting).

2. At one time the whole family was exposed to death: grandparents lived nearby or in the homes with their families. Grandchildren would often help care for their dying grandparents. Today, however, with death usually taking place not in the home but in the hospital or nursing home, family members may not be exposed to death. Even if the dying person is in the home, the family (children and grandchildren) may not be present. Families may live miles and even states away.

3. Because of the low infant mortality rate in our society, children are not exposed to the death of siblings as were children a hundred years ago.

4. Advances in medical science have encouraged us to think that all ills can be cured or will be cured in our lifetime.

5. Our growing technological control over our world has led us to feel uncomfortable with anything that we cannot control. Death appears as a contra-

diction to our "self-appointed" role as the masters of our destiny, therefore we do our best to deny it.

6. Along with #5 above, with our reliance more on technology than on God for our destinies, and life less harsh than previous generations, the consolation of a spiritual and physical immortality has been eroded.

Do you agree that the subject of death and dying is rarely discussed in church? Why or why not?_____

_____

_____

_____

_____

_____

Biblical Understanding of Death

While life after death is not a central consideration of the Old Testament, life after death did become a central doctrine of the Christian faith after the resurrection of Jesus. For the early Israelites, "life after death" came by having children and the continuance of their nation (an example is Abraham and Sarah and the birth of Isaac in Genesis 18).

Throughout the ages, there have been three prominent views regarding death:

1. Death as Extinction. At the point of death, life ceases to exist. There is no more life or afterlife. Death is the end.
2. Death as Reincarnation (or transmigration). According to this belief, often found in eastern religions, at death the soul is reincarnated or transmigrates to a higher or lower living creature on this earth. After death a person may become an insect, cow, or king. Our behavior in this life destines our body in the next.
3. Death as Transition or Resurrection. Death provides the opportunity for a self-conscious existence beyond this life. The essence of personhood lives on in a new realm: heaven.

As Christians, we believe that life exists beyond death. That death does not have the last word and we can boldly proclaim with Paul, "Death has been swallowed up in victory. Where, O death, is your victory? Where, O death, is your sting?" (Romans 15:54-55)

In order for us to have a better understanding of what the Bible says about death and resurrection, it is helpful for us to look at various biblical texts. "The Lord God formed man from the dust of the ground, and breathed into his nostrils the breath of life; and the man became a living being" (Genesis 2:7), and the Psalmist says that when God takes "away their breath, they die and return to their dust" (Psalm 104:29). Thus, at the core of the biblical understanding of death is the fact that both life and death are part of God's created order.

On occasion, death appears to be regarded as what we would call "natural," that is after having lived a life "full of days" (Job 42:17) or "full of years" (Genesis 25:8). At other times, death may seem to come too soon and to the young, "and suddenly a great wind came across the desert, struck the four corners of the house, and it fell on the young people, and they are dead" (Job 1:19).

The biblical account is clear that God intended humankind to enjoy life forever, even as God does. "God created humankind in his image, in the image of God he created them" (Genesis 1:17). But, "by man came death" (1 Corinthians 15:21). Because of humankind's disobedience God drove man and woman from the Garden of Eden before they could "take also from the tree of life, and eat, and live forever" (Genesis 3:22). From this point on, humankind dies because of sin. Aging is part of life and death and is God's judgment on humankind. Such becomes in the Bible the primary meaning of sin, "for the wages of sin is death" (Romans 6:23).

Yet God's purposes in the world and for humankind could not be accomplished until the power of sin and death were destroyed. According to the persistent word of the New Testament, that is what God did in Christ. "Since, therefore, the children share flesh and blood, he himself likewise shared the same things, so that through death he might destroy the one who has the power of death, that is the devil, and free those who all their lives were held in slavery by the fear of death" (Hebrews 2:14-15).

Indeed for Christians, we have already died the death that robs death of its prey. As it is written: "But if we have died with Christ, we believe that we will also live with him. We know that Christ, being raised from the dead, will never die again; death no longer has dominion over him" (Romans 6:8-9). Further, "if the Spirit of him who raised Jesus from the dead dwells in you, he who raised Christ from the dead will give life to your mortal bodies also through his Spirit that dwells in you" (Romans 8:11).

The biblical understanding of death is really a function of its understanding of God. And here God is by definition the one "who gives life to the dead and calls into existence the things that do not exist" (Romans 4:17). God is the one "who did not withhold his own Son, but gave him up for all of us" (Romans 8:32). It is God who said "Behold, I make all things new . . . . I am the Alpha and the Omega, the beginning and the end" (Revelation 21:5-6). In this faith, it is appropriate to say, "Death shall be no more" (Revelation 21:4).

The traditional view of Christianity is that those who believe will share eternally the bliss of fellowship with God in heaven, while those who refuse God's love are eternally separated from God. In general the New Testament seems to suggest that life after death is a continuation of life before death, but on what may be called a "spiritual level." In this sense, eternal life is something that is given here and continues after death. If we grow in grace, in love, and in knowledge of God here, it shall continue afterward. If we are in rebellion here, then we shall continue to experience separation in death.

Jesus proclaimed, "I am the resurrection and the life. Those who believe in me, even though they die, will live, and everyone who lives and believes in me will never die" (John 11:25-26).

Can you identify other Scripture passages that relate to our understanding of death?

_____

_____

_____

_____

End-of-Life Planning: Advance Directives

As we read in Chapter 2 on health and aging, medical advances have contributed significantly to the aging of our population. Lives are prolonged with the arrival of new technologies, equipment, drugs, and treatments, including:

- Ventilators to provide artificial respiration
- Feeding tubes
- Defibrillators to restart a heart
- Immediate medical attention at accidents by EMS technicians

But such advances in medicine and pharmacology also have another effect: prolonging life to a state of vulnerable frailty, somewhere between living and dying.

Many readers will recall the Terri Schiavo situation. A young woman collapsed in her home and experienced respiratory and cardiac arrest. She suffered brain damage and became dependent on a feeding tube, which led to 15 years of institutionalization and a diagnosis of persistent vegetative state. Terri had never made any end-of-life plans and did not prepare an advance directive. In an effort by her husband to have life-support equipment removed, Terri's family was torn apart, and both the state and federal governments became involved in the decision-making process, including: the governor of the state of Florida, the Florida Supreme Court, the United States Congress, and the President. Unfortunately, this tragic situation became a circus and a spectacle in our society.

To help us in our thinking about end-of-life planning, we would do well to remember these words from Scripture: "For everything there is a season, and a time for every matter under heaven: a time to be born, and a time to die" (Ecclesiastes 3:1-2).

Pastors and other church leaders often fail to discuss end-of-life planning with parishioners in part because they assume medical doctors are doing this. Unfortunately, physicians may be reluctant to discuss end-of-life planning, too. Believing that the Hippocratic Oath places all emphasis on keeping someone alive, death may be seen as an inappropriate outcome.

Another reason doctors as well as pastors and church leaders ignore end-of-life planning with patients and church members is because they themselves have not dealt with their own end-of-life planning, and therefore lack training in this process.

And, finally, both doctors and pastors may be uncomfortable with death and may even fear their own death. As a result, they are reluctant to talk about end-of-life planning with others as a way of avoiding death itself.

Unfortunately, older adults often wait for their pastor or medical doctor to initiate such discussions rather than making the first moves themselves. Sometimes it isn't until an older person needs hospitalization, or worse yet, a critical situation occurs and the issue of end-of-life planning becomes a reality.

Our discussion of end-of-life planning will center on advance directives. I believe that it is fundamentally important for church leaders engaged in older adult ministry to become knowledgeable about end-of-life planning, especially as it involves advance directives. However, it should be noted that advance directives are but one piece of end-of-life planning. Other important elements include: Will or trust document (to pass on property), durable power of attorney (for financial affairs), organ donor cards, and funeral or burial plans.

A helpful definition of advance directive: Advance directive is a witnessed, written document or oral statement wherein a competent adult leaves instructions concerning any aspect of his/her health care in the event he/she is ever incapacitated. It provides for a substitute decision maker and identifies desired medical treatments. An advance directive is made up of two elements:

- Living will
- Durable power of attorney for health care

Living Will

A living will is generally invoked when a person is considered terminal. A living will allows older adults to express their wishes regarding withdrawal, withholding, or provision of life-prolonging procedures. It refers to any medical procedure, treatment, or intervention that uses mechanical or other artificial means to sustain, restore, or supplant vital functioning and when applied to a patient in terminal condition serves only to prolong the process of dying.

A living will outlines the type of care a patient would want or would reject in the terminal stage. It can only be acted upon if a patient is suffering from a terminal condition or a permanent and irreversible state of unconsciousness (a persistent vegetative state) or if the patient is incapacitated and there is no reasonable probability that the patient will recover capacity (so that he/she may exercise own right to make a decision directly).

Typical living will language simply states the desire that life-prolonging procedures be withheld or withdrawn in the event of a terminal condition. However, when preparing a living will, it is important to keep in mind that providing explicit directions such as "do not resuscitate" rather then a generic phrase like "no heroic measures" can be more helpful in providing clear guidance.

Durable Power of Attorney for Health Care

A durable power of attorney is distinct from a living will in that a health care directive is not limited to the terminal state, while a living will is generally invoked when a person is considered terminal. In addition, a durable power of attorney for health care document may need to be witnessed, and depending upon your state's legal requirements, notarized.

A durable power of attorney is a legal document naming an agent, called a proxy or surrogate, to be a substitute decision-maker when a patient is incompetent. A proxy can be a spouse, adult child, friend, or relative, but should live nearby. Most important, this person should know the senior's values, religious beliefs, and wishes regarding medical treatment, organ donation, and nursing home placement. If the patient has not designated someone to make decisions regarding medical treatment in the event they become incapacitated, a court-appointed guardian may be named.

If an older adult becomes incapacitated, it will be the decision of the proxy that matters as to the best interests of the patient. The older adult should communicate fully with the proxy concerning expressed preferences regarding the use, or withholding, of any specific treatment or procedures, as well as relevant religious beliefs and personal values, long before any possible emergency.

Older adults wanting to execute an advance directive should be encouraged to seek the assistance of a knowledgeable health care provider, pastor, social worker, or attorney. Keep in mind that each state provides for its own rules and regulations concerning advance directives.

Some questions for further reflection regarding death:

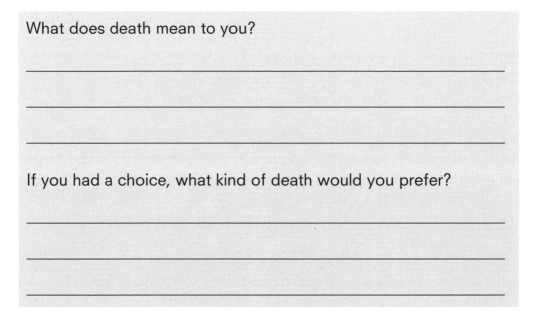

What does death mean to you?

_____

_____

_____

If you had a choice, what kind of death would you prefer?

_____

_____

_____

If you could choose, when and where would you die?

_____

_____

_____

Increasingly, medical treatments can add years to life without providing a cure. Do you believe some conditions are worse than
death? Why or why not?

_____

_____

_____

When is quality of life more important than longevity?

_____

_____

_____

Who would you choose to be your durable power of attorney for
health care? Why?

_____

_____

_____

_____

Ministry and Aging

In our youth-oriented society, the image of an aging congregation is that of a burdensome and closed-minded mausoleum that exists steadfastly in tradition and all too often hinders church growth. With such negative thinking, is it any wonder that many pastors enter retirement with a great sense of failure and guilt because they failed to "grow young churches?" Such an attitude reflects an assumption that church growth is only valid when there are increasing numbers of people under 35 years of age, not increasing numbers of people at any age and all ages.

Stated previously in the Introductory Chapter, the purpose of this book is to help church leaders to reflect on various issues of aging and older adulthood and to provide the resources necessary for developing intentional ministry by, with, and for older adults. In this chapter, we will discuss the organizational structure needed for a comprehensive ministry to take place.

As we reflect on older adult ministry, it is helpful to keep in mind that the purpose of the church is to make disciples of Jesus Christ. Thus our efforts in older adult ministry are:

- to nurture faith by acknowledging both the blessings and the losses of later life and recognizing that interdependence, not independence, is of greater value.
- to build Christian community by developing a structure in our churches that encourages and facilitates intentional ministry by, with, and for older adults.

- to equip older adults for faithful living and service by offering a fresh perspective, one that sees older adults as active participants in contributing to the church's life and mission and in meeting the spiritual needs of its members.

Comprehensive Ministry

In the book, *The Graying of the Church*, a comprehensive plan for congregational ministries with older adults called S.E.N.I.O.R.S. Ministry was provided. S.E.N.I.O.R.S. Ministry is an acronym for **S**pirituality, **E**nrichment, **N**utrition, **I**ntergenerational, **O**utreach, **R**ecreation, and **S**ervice. (*The Graying of the Church: A Leader's Guide to Older Adult Ministry in The United Methodist Church* by Richard H. Gentzler, Jr. [Nashville: Discipleship Resources, 2004] pp. 37-44) Intentional ministry by, with, and for older adults should include specific ministry in each of these areas. Very briefly:

- Spirituality is ministry in some or all of the following: worship, Sunday school classes, Bible study groups, prayer groups, spiritual retreats and journaling, healing services, end-of-life issues, and support groups.
- Enrichment involves learning opportunities and classroom seminars on topics of interest to older adults such as finances, advance directives, legal issues, computers and the internet, life review and reminiscence, and book clubs.
- Nutrition/Wellness involves congregational health ministries, parish nurse ministry, low impact aerobics and other forms of exercise, cooking classes (i.e., low-fat, low-sodium, cooking for one), and nutritious meals.
- Intergenerational creates intentional ministry in multi-generational settings such as retreats, vacation Bible school, Bible studies, Sunday school classes, Puppet and clown ministry, tutoring children, and mentoring adults.
- Outreach ministry involves intentional evangelistic efforts in reaching older adults in the community, as well as inviting older adults to be involved in outreach to others of all ages.
- Recreation ministry involves play and leisure activities and might include board games, fellowship meals, travel events and field trips, scavenger hunts, and fishing and golfing outings.
- Service ministry invites older adults to be involved in various skill levels including long- or short-term mission projects, transportation, visitation, respite care, home chore services and minor home repairs.

This brief summary gives you an idea how comprehensive a S.E.N.I.O.R.S.

Ministry can be in a congregation or as an intentional ministry with a cluster of smaller congregations all working together for the well-being of older members.

In Chapter 3, on retirement and aging, we looked at the three phases of retirement: Active (Go-Go phase), Passive (Slow-Go phase), and Final (No-Go phase). Appendix B, provides you with a helpful tool (the S.E.N.I.O.R.S. Ministry Grid) which invites you to assess the areas of S.E.N.I.O.R.S. Ministry already taking place in your congregation. Each area of ministry of this model invites the reader to look at Spirituality, Enrichment, Nutrition/Wellness, Intergenerational, Outreach, Recreation, and Service with three specific groups of older adults: the Go-Go's, the Slow-Go's, and the No-Go's. Meeting with several others in your congregation, review the ministry in your congregation and identify the specific programs you have in each area for each of these three groups of older adults. Then, apply this information to the grid. As you review the S.E.N.I.O.R.S. Ministry Grid, answer the following questions:

In what areas of ministry is your church most heavily involved and with which group of people? Identify the top three ministry areas that you are reaching the most number of older adults.

_____

_____

_____

_____

What areas of ministry is your church the least involved in with ministry with older adults? Identify the three ministry areas that you are least engaged in ministry with older adults.

_____

_____

_____

_____

Can you identify ways to increase your ministry in areas that you are least engaged in ministry with older adults? What are they?

_____

_____

_____

Barriers to Older Adult Ministry

As we begin designing an intentional ministry by, with, and for older adults, it is important for leaders to reflect on some of the barriers that hinder effective ministry with older adults. Several barriers include:

1. *The church lacks a compelling vision for later life.* Most people just can't walk out their door and make a difference. There needs to be someplace to go, a well-developed avenue to help channel goodwill into good deeds. Congregations are all too often focused on keeping the "old folks" busy rather than on accomplishing a ministry of genuine significance.

2. *The ministry is not considered "important" by church leadership.* When a church adds a new staff person it is most often a youth or children's director, seldom is a staff person added in older adult ministry (unless it is a visitation minister). As a result, other ministry options are given higher priority, funding, and staff time.

3. *The ministry may not have the "right" people around the table.* In other words, people may be named to an older adult ministry committee, team, or task force, but have no idea, other than their age, why they are there. The pastor or someone else asked them to serve, but they have no vision or "calling" for ministry with older adults and they have no "job training" for what is expected of them.

4. *The ministry may fail because there is no structure or process in place.* If older adult ministry is "done" it is up to one person to it. There is no shared vision and no committee involvement in ministry. People expect someone else to do ministry. No one assumes responsibility or becomes accountable.

5. *Older adults, themselves, may be an obstacle to an older adult ministry.* They may reflect the pervasive "ageist" attitude in society and feel that older adults are

"too old" and "over-the-hill" for ministry or that ministry should be directed toward young people only.

6. *The church may not be accessible.* Restroom locations, stairways, poor lighting and acoustics may be some of the many features in church facilities that prevents meaningful ministry with older adults to occur.

Can you identify other barriers to older adult ministry in the church? If so, what are they?

_____

_____

_____

_____

Can you identify barriers that may exist in your church situation? What are they?

_____

_____

_____

_____

Can you identify ways to overcome the barriers in your church?

_____

_____

_____

_____

Overcoming these barriers may not be insurmountable, but they do require work. Being able to identify barriers is the first step in the process. Because of your leadership role, you may well be instrumental in helping to overcome the barriers that exist in your church.

Getting Started

Step 1: *Establish an older adult ministry committee, team, or task force.* Find one or two people in your church who have a concern for older adults. Meet during breakfast or lunch and talk freely about your vision for ministry. Think about other people in your church or community who might share your vision and plan to meet with them. Bring together a group of six to eight people (most of whom should be older adults) who share in a vision for older adult ministry in your church. Then, approach your pastor or church council, and get permission to become a ministry committee, team, or task force.

The role of a local church committee, council or team should include, but not be limited to, the following:

- Advocate on behalf of older adults and older adult concerns
- Focus on the Mission and Vision of your local church
- Identify needs and talents of older adults
- Survey existing church programs and facilities
- Implement S.E.N.I.O.R.S. Ministry, an intentional ministry model that includes spirituality, enrichment, nutrition/wellness, intergenerational, outreach, recreation, and service
- Network with community, district, and conference leaders and resources

Step 2: *Conduct a survey of older adults in your church.* Before a comprehensive ministry can begin, you will want to know who the older adults are in your congregation and community. Discovering their needs, as well as their gifts or talents for ministry, is a vital step in developing older adult ministry. We can not presume to know the needs and talents of the older adults in our congregation. We must first ask. And, discovering who the older adults are who live in our community is an excellent opportunity for the church to become more involved in the life of the community.

Develop a survey instrument for gathering information about the older adults in your church. In designing a survey form, obtain the following information: (1) name of older adult, his or her address, telephone number, email address, and other general information, (2) needs and concerns of the older adult, and (3) ways older adults can serve the needs of others. In Appendices C and D, you will find two different types of survey forms. Older Adult Survey—Sample 1 is a typical survey form that invites older adults to respond according to their needs and talents. Older Adult Survey—Sample 2 is slightly different and invites older adults to share more of themselves, as well as their interests and opinions. You will want to review these two forms with the help of your committee or team, and then design an Older Adult Survey form that best fits your needs.

It is important to know as much about the older adults in your congregation and community as possible. Be thorough in asking the right questions. After you have developed the survey form, you will want to interview all the older adults in your congregation (and community, if feasible).

Before taking your survey, invite your pastor to send a letter to older adults and to place announcements in the weekly bulletin and/or congregation newsletter explaining the survey and interview process. Invite older adults to receive into their homes a trained interviewer who will share the questionnaire with them. You may also want to survey larger groups of older adults at one time. For example, one or more interviewers could visit an older adult Sunday school class and conduct the survey on a Sunday morning.

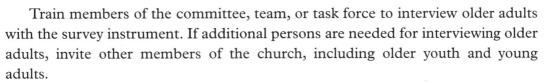

Identify other ways you can conduct a survey with older adults.

Train members of the committee, team, or task force to interview older adults with the survey instrument. If additional persons are needed for interviewing older adults, invite other members of the church, including older youth and young adults.

Conduct a training session with all members of the committee, team, or task force who will be using the survey instrument. Interviewers will need to learn about the procedures you decide for interviewing older adults, including information about: being prompt in visiting the survey participant at the agreed upon day and time; introducing themselves and showing identification, if necessary, and stating why they are there; giving the older adult being interviewed a copy of the survey form; asking each question on the form and writing or printing each answer clearly; not over-extending their stay past 20-30 minutes in length; maintaining eye contact and a speaking voice that is warm and friendly and inviting; making certain that distractions in the room are minimized (e.g., television or radio off or turned down low); maintaining confidentiality on personal matters that might be shared; thanking the participant for taking time to complete the survey; and finally, indicating what you want the interviewer to do with survey instrument once it has been completed.

Some simple steps for conducting an older adult survey include:

1. Design your survey instrument or questionnaire
2. Decide who will do the interviewing and who will train the interviewers
3. Determine the people to be surveyed (e.g., people 65 and older, church members or the whole community)
4. Announce plans for conducting the survey to the church
5. Select interview teams of two people each
6. Decide who will train the teams of interviewers
7. Select a time and place to train the interviewers
8. Select a person or team to collect completed survey forms
9. Enter information into a database
10. Have committee, team or task force review data for ministry options

Are there additional steps you would take in conducting an older adult survey with the members of your church and community? If so, what are they?

_____

_____

_____

_____

Step 3: *Review existing church programs that already involve older adults.* Are older adults already involved in particular ministries in the church? Do they sing in the choir, teach in the Sunday school, provide leadership on various church committees, participate in mission trips and work projects? Are they participating in Bible study groups, women's and men's fellowship groups, and shepherding new members?

Look around your church; identify existing programs that already involve older adults.

_____

Now, identify any existing programs in your church in which older adults are not involved, but could be. What are they?

_____

_____

_____

_____

Are there ways you could involve older adults in these existing programs?

_____

_____

_____

_____

Step 4: *Conduct a demographic and service analysis of your community.* In addition to knowing the needs and talents of older adults in your church, you will want to become aware of the older adult population in your community. Less than 50%

of older adults are involved in the church, and with growing numbers of aging Baby Boomers, the number of older adults having no church affiliation will likely increase. It is helpful to have a fresh perspective of the older adults in your community.

A good way to get a clear picture of the older adults and their needs in your community is by becoming aware of existing programs in your community for older adults. Visit the social service agencies your community and ask questions about the projects and programs for older adults. A good place to start is with your local Office on Aging or the Area Agency on Aging. Staff in these agencies can provide you with helpful information.

In addition to knowing what is already available for older adults, ask the social service agencies to identify areas of unmet need. It may be possible that the services needed could be provided by your congregation or by several congregations working together.

You might ask, "Who in our community can we partner with in order to provide a comprehensive older adult ministry?" "What other churches and social service agencies can we work with in our effort to provide an intentional ministry by, with, and for older adults?"

As a result of your local church survey and your investigation of community services, you should have a clear and thorough understanding of both met and unmet needs of older adults in your church and community.

Step 5: *Plan ministry events targeted to older adults, both inside and outside the church.* After you have analyzed the data from your interviews with the older adults in your congregation and have identified community social service agency programs, your committee, team, or task force will be ready to begin planning a specific ministry with older adults.

Ideas for ministry will surface from the various surveys and interviews. You might find that your older adults need transportation to and from church or that a respite care ministry is desired. A parish nurse ministry or mid-week Bible study might be needed. After you evaluate your survey information, you will need to prioritize a list of ideas. You may have too many issues to address all at once. By prioritizing your list, you will be able to begin ministry with the greatest need or concern.

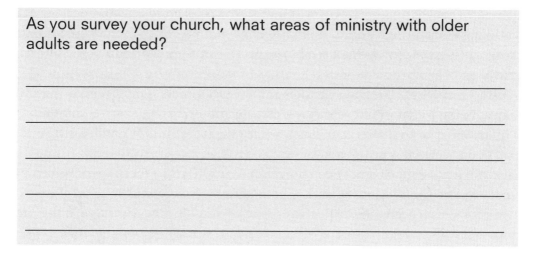

As you survey your church, what areas of ministry with older adults are needed?

_____

_____

_____

_____

_____

Advocates for Older Adult Ministries

As the church begins developing intentional ministries with older adults, you will want to have ministry "advocates" or "champions" to help guide the ministry projects. The task of the ministry advocate is to oversee a particular or specialized ministry project, someone who will take responsibility for seeing that the ministry is actually carried out. The advocate should have both an understanding of and a passion for older adult ministry. Unless a particular ministry has an advocate to see it through, the committee, team or task force should go no further with the project. Only those ministry ideas that have an advocate should proceed.

Once an advocate is named, it becomes the responsibility of that person to make certain the ministry is carried forward. The ministry advocate will work with a team in planning for the particular ministry. Regular reports by the team and ministry advocate will be presented to the full committee. The ministry advocate will provide an assessment of the ministry at regular intervals and will present a final evaluation after the ministry project is completed.

If you are the ministry advocate, begin by establishing a timeline for implementing your ministry project. Identify the various steps along the way. Make a flowchart to help you identify and understand the process involved in your specific ministry project. List the resources to be used (both materials and personnel) and the outcome you want to achieve. This is your check list, or memory jog, as you implement your ministry. It will help you make sure your vision for older adult ministries is being realized.

Step 6: *Evaluate.* Periodically evaluate the program to make sure you are accomplishing what you set out to achieve. This is a good way to determine the effectiveness of your older adult ministry. Listen to the voices of the people you are serving. Are they receiving the desired results? Is your ministry making a difference in the lives of older adults and in the life of your church? Are there gaps in the process? Are persons growing in their faith development and spiritual maturity? Are lives being transformed as a result of your ministry?

In an effort to evaluate your older adult ministries, **learn how to listen**. Use surveys, one-on-one conversations, focus groups, event evaluations, and other means for getting feedback. The more information you receive, the better your chances will be for developing and implementing a viable and successful ministry that meets and exceeds the expectations of persons involved in your older adult ministry.

Periodically, perhaps annually, you will want to survey the older adults in your congregation. Life needs change and any effective older adult ministry must keep informed of the changes affecting the lives of older adults. In addition, you will want have regular contact with the social service agencies in your community. Keeping abreast of aging issues and older adult events in your community is important for maximizing the effectiveness of your ministry.

Quality is important to any consumer. Continuous improvement is vital to the success of business. Likewise, congregations need to be aware of the importance of quality in meeting the needs of the people. As you receive feedback, continue to improve your ministry program. If you discover, through feedback, that a specific ministry is not working, begin the process over again.

For a more comprehensive understanding of designing an older adult ministry in your congregation, you will want to read *Designing an Older Adult Ministry* by Richard H. Gentzler, Jr. [Nashville: Discipleship Resources, 1999] pp. 31-44.

From Faith to Practice: SAGE Corps

Older adulthood has the potential to become the best stage of life, an age of liberation when older adults combine newfound freedoms with prolonged health. It can be a time when individuals make their most important contributions to life, faith, society, and the world. Unfortunately, many older adults lament the loss of usefulness after retirement. Some see this stage of life as an "elder wasteland"

In Psalms we read, "Even to old age and gray hairs, O God, do not forsake me, until I proclaim your might to all the generations to come" (Psalm71:18). As I reflect on this desire of the psalmist to proclaim God's might (e.g., love, power, faith, and grace) to succeeding generations, I can only imagine what such a vision would look like if congregations were truly intentional in helping older adults find meaning and worth in the later years.

If in fact as we age we have the opportunity to grow in wisdom, to gain experience, and to deepen our faith, to what end or purpose does all this have? Is it beneficial for Christians to watch 48 hours of television a week, which is roughly the average for older adults? Will playing 18 holes of golf several days a week add meaning and purpose to the life of an older adult? There isn't necessarily anything wrong with watching television or playing golf, and many people anxiously look forward to retirement so they can enjoy more leisure time; however, if people are living longer and healthier than previous generations, what purpose does living longer have for individuals and for our world?

Perhaps it's time for congregations to invite "prime-timers" to really put faith into practice by creating intentional opportunities for older adults to live out their Christian discipleship in service to others. An example of this ministry might be called "SAGE Corps": **S**piritually **A**ctive **G**enerative **E**lders. More than a fellowship group or an "eatin' & meetin'" program, SAGE Corps models Christian "elderhood" in our world today. Rather than thinking of old age as a vast wasteland, SAGE Corps members seek to serve Christ in all things and with all people.

What would it mean for the revitalization of our churches if we started a SAGE Corps among older adults? If congregations were to mobilize our older men and older women, organize them to confront the ills of our society, send them out in pairs like the original disciples, we could change the face of this land. Our times demand just such a ministry.

As an intentional ministry, SAGE Corps could tap into the existing programs of women's groups and men's groups, or it could be a wholly new ministry with older adults reaching out to all generations. It would engage evangelism and nurture teams, and older adults would be equipped and empowered for mission, service, and outreach.

Older adults often have the necessary experience for serving in ways that are unique, meaningful, and life changing. The church should be one of the best sources for volunteers to serve in their communities and beyond.

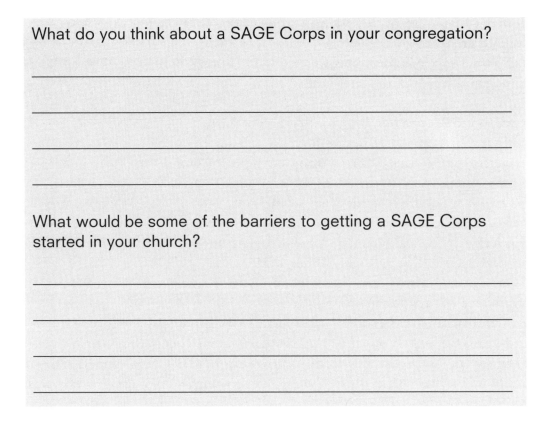

What do you think about a SAGE Corps in your congregation?

What would be some of the barriers to getting a SAGE Corps started in your church?

Some examples for community service that older adults can do include: home visitation; deliver "meals on wheels", provide home maintenance and handyman services, offer caregivers support and respite, provide tutoring in local schools, serve meals in homeless shelters, and mentor parents and young married couples. Examples of mission service for older adults include short-term and long-term mission experiences. Most church denominations have opportunities for older adults to use their many skills in the mission field both nationally and around the world.

What would be some of the types of ministry SAGE Corps members could be involved in your congregation?

In order to bring about such a corps of people in the service to Christ and the church, there needs to be some guiding principles. These principles would include:

Name: The SAGE Corps name is a deliberate attempt to avoid names associated with age (e.g., Elder Corps or Senior Corps), and to honor the sturdy, widely possessed, unintimidating assets present in many older adults: Wisdom and Experience. An acronym for SAGE can mean: S-spiritually A-active G-generative E-elders.

Impact: SAGE Corps would engage real problems of major significance in our communities and in the world. Older adults, growing in faith and spiritual maturity, would be involved in advocacy for all God's children at every age and stage of life. Older adults, invited to grow as disciples of Jesus Christ, would be empowered for making a difference in the lives of individuals (people of all ages), communities, and the world.

Commitment: Joining the SAGE Corps would require a major commitment for older adults for a defined period of time. For some people, the commitment would be to become involved in community service projects for a lengthy period of time. For others, the commitment might be for a shorter duration and in various parts of the world. Many older adults are already involved in wonderful mission work around the world, and in various regions of the country. Often, however, mission and service opportunities can also be met in an individual's local community.

Deployment: SAGE Corps members would be deployed in sufficient concentration to be a presence wherever they are serving, whether locally, regionally, or throughout the world. Teams would be created for mutual support, encouragement, and experience.

Leadership: SAGE Corps members would provide initiative, creativity, and leadership. Leadership would be named by the church council and officers selected by SAGE Corps members. Leadership need would be dependent upon the specific mission and service involvement and the duration of the specific ministry. Each SAGE Corps team would have a leader who would supervise the activities and ministry of the corps.

Spiritual Growth and Learning: Members of SAGE Corps would practice spiritual disciplines (e.g., daily prayer and Bible study, regular attendance in worship, and Christian conferencing) and be engaged in acquiring new experiences and gaining new knowledge.

Diversity: SAGE Corps would be open to everyone over a certain age as determined by the needs and numbers of older adults in your local church. Most SAGE Corps members would be 65 years of age or older, but some congregations might have SAGE Corps members as young as 50 or 55. Some might question the wisdom of using chronological age as a basis for membership in the SAGE Corps movement. Perhaps one reason for doing so is to provide an opportunity for people at midlife and older to be intentional in ministry and service.

Recognizing that many older adults are already involved as Christian disciples helping to meet the needs of children, youth and adults in their communities and throughout the world, SAGE Corps can be a creative way of putting faith into practice in an intentional, comprehensive ministry. SAGE Corps can be a critical venture for revitalizing congregations and communities. Members would engage in listening to the needs and then help in finding ways of meeting those needs. SAGE Corps can be adapted and designed to meet the needs of various levels of skills and abilities of older adults.

Again, the question is raised, "What is the purpose of living longer if it is not to fulfill the purpose of God?" SAGE Corps is a way of inviting older adults to engage in spiritual growth and for organizing older adults to be in service to the needs of others. SAGE Corps is an intentional ministry that engages older adults in Christian discipleship. Through this model of Christian elderhood, older adults have an opportunity for finding meaning and purpose in the later years. They will experience the reality of the psalmist's yearning by "proclaiming God's might to all the generations."

What do you think about SAGE Corps? Do you already have such a ministry in your congregation, perhaps by another name? If so, what is your ministry?

_____

_____

_____

If not, is there a way you can create a SAGE Corps ministry with older adults in your congregation?

_____

_____

Identify several people who could be good leaders for starting a SAGE Corps ministry in your church?

CHAPTER
8

Boomers and Aging

The Boomer Generation

In the 1960s and 70s young people protested the Vietnam War, burned their draft cards and their bras, marched on Washington, started a sexual revolution, founded Earth Day, and vowed never to trust anyone over the age of 30! Now many of those same young people are in their 60's and are steadily approaching older adulthood.

Following the aftermath of World War II, our country (and many others) experienced a surge in births. Between 1946 and 1964, approximately 78 million babies were born in the United States. Demographers labeled them the Baby Boomers. Their sheer numbers made them a force to reckon with as they moved through the earliest phases of their collective life. They overwhelmed the resources of local school districts and outgrew Sunday school classrooms. They created their own youth culture around music and clothing and aggressively acted out against their elders' social norms around sex, race, gender, and authority.

At the dawn of the 21st Century, the first wave of Boomers became 55 years of age. Now, 8,000 Boomers turn 60 everyday. By 2011, the oldest Boomer will reach 65. When the Boomer generation becomes 65 years of age and older, the older population in the United States will more than double from 35 million in 2000 to 72 million in 2030. With the Boomer generation fast approaching the traditional age of older adulthood, it is important for church leaders to have a clear understanding of this aging population. The Boomer generation will impact and change how we do ministry with older adults.

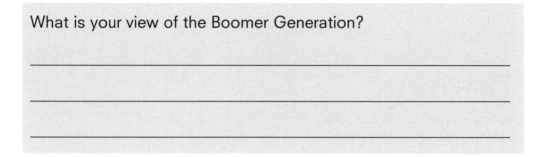

What is your view of the Boomer Generation?

The massive postwar Boomer generation has changed cultural trends for 60 years—from Howdy Doody to the Beatles, from leisure suits to jeans, from "dress for success" to "dress down Fridays." Boomers are at the top and the bottom of the socio-economic scale. Some are CEOs and professionals. To date, two presidents have been elected from their ranks: Bill Clinton and George W. Bush. Others are technicians, housewives, and laborers. Many are still working, others are retirees or unemployed, and some are homeless. They are single, married, parents, divorced, new parents, empty nesters, widowed, college students, and grandparents. It is important to remember that while we are talking about the Boomer generation, there is no single Boomer identity per se. In other words, "one size does not fit all." There aren't "Boomers" who fit every description, interest, habit, plan or activity attributed to them by the media. Just because they are aging doesn't mean that they can be neatly lumped into one homogeneous group.

As Boomers have cycled through their various life stages they passed through "hippie" and "yuppie" to become "abbies": aging baby boomers! But don't tell Boomers they're aging. Most don't want to be thought of as getting older. Don't label them "seniors," "senior citizens," or "older adults." Boomers don't want to be identified with anything that is old. Many Boomers are doing everything they can to keep themselves from getting old: participating in regular exercise, eating health foods, taking vitamins and using creams, and making "retirement" sound like a four-letter word. They really do expect to stay young and see getting old as an option, rather than as a reality.

Perhaps much of the hype about Boomer youthfulness is being driven by the multi-billion dollar a year anti-aging industry. After all, anti-aging medicine and other products have much to gain from such a large Boomer population. And, since Boomers don't want to look old, feel old, or seem old, the anti-aging industry is more than willing to help in this effort. Aging might not be something Boomers want to do, but as living, breathing creatures they will in time "come of age."

Boomers are healthier, more educated, and wealthier than any previous generation, and more inclined to stay in the workforce. Many Boomers plan to work well past traditional retirement age, but not always with their current employers. Boomers are "adventurers," always looking for that next thrill. As they become "empty-nesters," Boomers will engage in new experiences from going back to college and starting new careers to redefining community life and experimenting with the latest technology. If Boomers think about aging at all, it is their belief that a new aging culture will replace aging stereotypes of decline, disease, and dementia with empowering values of independence, activity, well-being, and mobility.

As Boomers go through the stages of growing older, they bring with them a unique historical profile, and they will have the opportunity to redefine the meaning and purpose of the older years. But it is equally important to remember that Boomers' basic needs are no different from those of previous generations. To the extent that Boomers appear different is mainly in how they *satisfy* their needs, not in what their needs *are*. For example, Boomers are just beginning to experience a new liberating phase of life, when they will shed past inhibitions and once again express themselves more freely.

Everywhere, people and organizations (including the church) are trying to figure out aging Boomers. They want to know what Boomers want as they move into the retirement years. Will they be involved in the life of the church? Will they embrace new dimensions of spirituality? Will they even attend church?

The place to begin our understanding of Boomer aging is to recognize that there are two distinct age-cohorts within the Boomer generation. The first age-cohort is often described as the "leading edge" or "early wave" of Boomers. They were the first of their generation born in 1946-1954. Their shared values and the impact culture had on their early lives are much different from their younger siblings "late Boomers," who were born in 1955-1964. The "leading edge" Boomers are the ones now in their mid-fifties and early sixties and are helping to create a new understanding of older adult ministry in the 21st century.

In this chapter, we will especially look at the commonalities leading edge Boomers share at comparable ages with other generations. They will share the same needs as their parents and their parents before them. What will be different is how Boomers express themselves in the culture in which they live.

The Generational Anchor Points Chart, found in Appendix C, is one lens through which you can see differences in how each of the older adult generations experienced life when they were youth and young adults. As you study this chart, please keep in mind that the lines between the generations are rather fluid. For example, people born in the early years of the Silent Generation (from 1926-1932) may have many of the same characteristics and values of the GI Generation. Likewise, persons born in the later years of the Silent Generation (from 1940-1945) may have many of the same characteristics and values of the "Leading Edge" Boomer Generation. Many factors determine such alignment including the age of parents and older siblings, as well as cultural influences.

Leading edge Boomers are beginning to realize that time passed and time left are no longer equal as they felt during midlife. Rather, they are beginning to measure time until death, rather than time from birth! Their self image is also beginning to change as a result of physical and biological changes. Some are caring for aging parents and many are adjusting to aging spouses.

As some of the demands of work and family that have held their attention recede, Boomers will have the potential to become an important resource of unprecedented proportions by actively participating in the life of their faith communities. But will they?

> Is your congregation reaching out to the Boomer Generation? If so, how?
>
> _____
>
> _____
>
> _____
>
> _____

Boomer Aging

"Will you still need me, will you still feed me when I'm sixty-four?" that was a question raised by the Beatles from their album "Sgt. Pepper's Lonely Heart's Club Band." While the Beatles might have been a bit too young in thinking 64 as the time of old age, they do raise an interesting question. Who will feed us, who will need us, when we are old?

It is impossible to predict Boomer aging with any degree of certainty. We can identify possibilities and traits, and possibly provide forecasts for the future. However, just as no one could have predicted life after 9/11 or the effects of New Orleans following Hurricane Katrina, neither can we predict how Boomers will age. It would be presumptuous for someone to say specifically how Boomers will age, and if they will age differently from previous generations. We simply do not know all the ramifications of our political, socio-economic, scientific, and global world.

We can, however, identify areas that Boomers will concern themselves with: their health and the cost of healthcare, work and retirement, and meaning and purpose in life. Such concerns will have an impact on Boomer's lives in ways that will perplex, trouble, and amaze them.

Health and Cost of Healthcare

While Boomers may hold higher standards for their health, engage in physical activity, and eat healthy foods, they are aging. And, with aging comes health decline. From obesity and diabetes to heart disease and cancer, Boomers are experiencing chronic conditions, which is affecting the way they live, work, and play.

Maintaining the quality of life with advancing age may not be easy for Boomers. With the decreasing birthrate in our country and more people living longer, there may be fewer workers. Who will provide healthcare? The supply of healthcare workers may not be sufficient to meet the demands of the large Boomer population. Businesses and politicians are already wrestling with the problems of healthcare cost and coverage.

In addition, the availability of family caregivers may also decrease as Boomers age. The reasons are many but include high divorce rates among the Boomer generation, late marriages, increasing childlessness and declining family sizes, and rising labor force participation of women. Boomers may have few, if any, family members to care for them in their old age.

As Boomers age and experience increasing health problems, so large a population could be crippling for the future Medicare costs, government financing of nursing home care, the nation's workforce needs and the caregiving burdens placed on their children. There is the very real possibility that Boomers who will live longer because of medical advances will spend many of their later years with increasing health problems and therefore experience greater healthcare costs.

On the flip side, with advances in medical technology and new discoveries in medicine, many Boomers believe that they will not experience the same negative effects in health as previous generations. They believe that wellness and prevention efforts, including changes in personal behavior such as diet, exercise, and not smoking, should be top priorities.

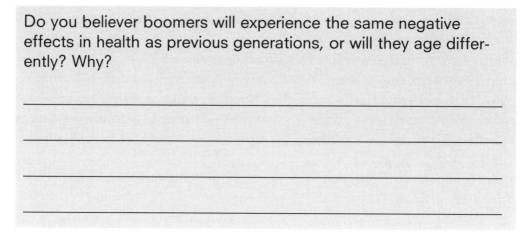

Do you believer boomers will experience the same negative effects in health as previous generations, or will they age differently? Why?

Retirement and Personal Finances

Ask Boomers if they plan to retire and many will say, "No." Boomers plan to change the concept of retirement as they age. As a result of better healthcare, job safety, medical technology, physical fitness, and a host of other variables, people are living longer and healthier today than ever before. If a 70-year old today is more like a 50-year old was 20 years ago, why not keep on working?

After all, work provides many important things:

- Structure—when to get up in the morning, where to go, how long to stay there, when to go home
- Community—a social fabric providing personal interaction
- Purpose—goals, meaning, focus, direction
- Income—wages and salary in order to live and pay bills (and for some, it also includes pension and healthcare benefits)

What does work mean to you?

Many Boomers do not plan to stop working and find the idea of retirement unthinkable. They have continuing career interests or want to stay productive. Many, however, will not achieve that goal. Health problems and workplace pressures such as cutbacks will force many Boomers into retirement earlier than they expect. And employers who have a choice often prefer the young, viewing older workers as costly and resistant to new technologies.

Many Boomers will continue to work not because they want to or because they find their job satisfying. Rather, they will do so because of lack of savings, dwindling retirement investments, or little or no pension funds. Traditional pension programs are becoming increasingly rare. Companies are cutting back on retiree healthcare benefits. Finding satisfying employment that provides for income security and healthcare benefits may become more difficult as Boomers age. There is also the fear of unstable Social Security coverage.

If Boomers have not saved adequately for retirement the incentive to work longer may increase in the years to come. Improvements in the health and longevity of Boomers and the less physically demanding nature of most jobs compared with those of past generations may also make it easier for Boomers to work longer than their predecessors. It is also possible that with fewer younger workers, employers may look differently at Boomers. As aging Boomers make their way into retirement and out of the work force, they may be leaving the company or organization with a huge brain drain and labor shortage. Employers may decide that the loss of experience and skill with Boomer retirement is too much to bear and decide to find ways of keeping Boomers in the workforce.

Perhaps the three major trends impacting the retirement future of Boomers are:

1. The shrinking or disappearance of corporate and government retirement benefits;
2. The rapid and unpredictable rise in healthcare costs;
3. Increased longevity.

Each of these trends may play a major role in the life of aging Boomers.

Do you agree or disagree with the view that Boomers will not retire? Why?

_____

_____

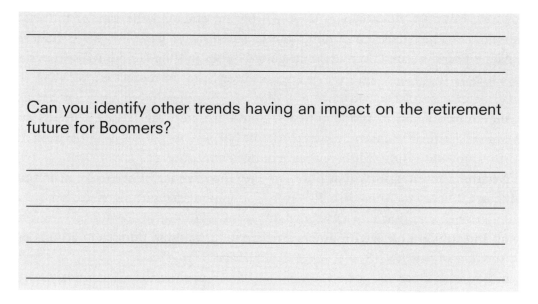

Can you identify other trends having an impact on the retirement future for Boomers?

Meaning and Purpose in Life

In addition to health and finances, having meaning or purpose in life is important for Boomers as they age. Feeling relevant in one's family and community, feeling that they are needed and making a positive contribution to their world, and feeling that they are still learning and growing are important for people of every generation. But where and how will Boomers find meaning and purpose in life as they age? Will it be different from previous generations?

Boomers might find meaning and purpose in life through a variety of opportunities, not least of which are:

- Positive relations with others
- Self-acceptance
- Personal Growth
- Autonomy
- Career/job satisfaction
- Spiritual growth

Since this is primarily a book for church leaders, I want to invite us to look at spiritual growth as it relates to Boomers and aging.

As Christians, we believe we can find meaning and purpose in our lives as revealed in the Great Commandment: You are to love the Lord your God with all your heart, soul, mind and strength; and, your neighbor as yourself. As I stated above, it isn't that the needs of Boomers are necessarily different from previous generations of aging adults; rather, the *way* they express their needs are different.

Many Boomers are "double boomerangs." They left the church when they were young only to return when they had school-age children. Now that their children have grownup and taken responsibility for their own lives, many Boomers are exiting the church again in the later years. Some are enjoying leisure pursuits such boating on the nearest lake or playing 18 holes of golf; while others are finding purpose and meaning through travel, personal growth, or work.

What is it about church that Boomers find unsatisfying? There have been many books and articles written about this topic, but no one seems to have a clear or prevailing idea. Certainly, many Boomers do find involvement in church life to be satisfying and fulfilling. Many Boomers participate in worship and study groups on a regular basis. They are involved in learning, service, and mission. They are reaching out to their neighbors and visiting the sick, homebound, and those in prisons. They are feeding the poor and sheltering the homeless. Many Boomers find meaning and purpose through their religious life. Others simply do not. For many Boomers, religious authority lies in the individual believer—rather than in the church or the Bible.

Can you identify barriers to Boomer church participation? What are they?

_____

_____

_____

_____

Reasons for Focusing Outreach on Boomers

There are several reasons that the church through its older adult ministry should focus on reaching Boomers:

- God loves Boomers
- Boomers are a large population
- Boomers make up a large number of non-church goers

- Boomers have both discretionary time and money
- Boomers want to be needed
- Boomers are in the "generative" years and want to help younger generations
- Boomers are facing many stressors that have an impact on their spiritual growth, such as:
  - Caring for aging parents or death of parents
  - Changes in work roles or transitioning to retirement
  - Changes in self-image as a result of physical or biological changes
  - Changes in family: empty nest, divorce, widowhood, grandparenting

Identify other reasons why churches should focus evangelism and outreach on the Boomer generation.

_____

_____

_____

While Boomers don't want to be called "seniors" and they don't want to be involved in traditional older adult ministries, many Boomers are searching for acceptance, authenticity, and honest engagement with life. If mainline churches can address these issues satisfactorily, Boomers are more likely to become involved.

Churches must keep in mind that aging Boomers may not know what they want to do or what they are able to do. Congregations that show a genuine interest in helping Boomers live more fulfilling and spiritual enriching lives will reap many benefits.

The question becomes, what can congregations do to help Boomers envision a life that achieves meaning and purpose by connecting in new ways to God and to the community around them?

Congregations can respond to aging Boomers by:

- Offering a variety of entry points where Boomers can meet others
- Develop activities that engage Boomers for their own sakes, not just for their kids
- Provide opportunities for meaningful service and mission, not just meetings

- Schedule activities that nurture the reflective life (prayer, meditation, journaling)
- Form small groups and support systems

Unless Boomers perceive opportunities for service as being convenient and tailored to their particular individual interests, they many not participate. A range of opportunities is needed to allow Boomers to engage in different ways at different times and at different levels of commitment.

What are the different opportunities your congregation provides for Boomers to become involved in ministry ?

_____

_____

_____

_____

Resources for Further Study and Reflection

Chapter 1: Myths, Realities, and Aging

Adult Aging and Development: Myths and Emerging Realities by Richard Schulz and Timothy Salthouse. Prentice-Hall (1999). This textbook covers topics such as health and aging, memory and learning, creativity and wisdom, stress and coping, physical and cognitive development, and personality and social development.

Aging: Concepts and Controversies by Harry R. Moody. Pine Forge Press, Thousand Oaks, CA (2000). An excellent resource that helps readers confront many of the issues impacting both aging persons and our aging society.

Aging Nation: The Economics and Politics of Growing Older in America by James H. Schulz and Robert H. Binstock. Praeger Publishers, Westport, CT (2006). A solid corrective look at the conventional (and often false) wisdom, propagated by the doomsters, about the perils of a nation living longer.

Graying Gracefully: Preaching to Older Adults edited by William J. Carl, Jr. Westminster John Knox Press (1997). This book provides practical, biblical and theological information relevant for understanding and preaching to the needs of older adults.

Living Old: The Modern Realities of Aging in America. WBGH Educational Foundation, PBS Home Video (2006). This video explores the realities of living longer lives and the unintended consequences of this new longevity.

Older Americans, Vital Communities: A Bold Vision for Societal Aging by W. Andrew Achenbaum. The Johns Hopkins University Press, Baltimore, MD (2005). A look at societal issues of aging.

The Power of the Dream by Marie White Webb. Abingdon Press, Nashville, TN (1999). A moving testimony of faithful living in the later years.

Chapter 2: Health and Aging

Ageless: Take Control of Your Age and Stay Youthful for Life by Edward L. Schneider, M.D. and Elizabeth Miles. Rodale (2003). This resource provides information on ways people can control their aging and significantly reduce their risk of disability and illness and feel vital and healthy throughout their lifespan.

Aging and God: Spiritual Pathways to Mental Health in Midlife and Later Years by Harold G. Koenig, MD. Haworth Press, New York (1994). The author argues convincingly that religious beliefs and practices make a positive difference in the lives of older adults.

The Art of Aging: A Doctor's Prescription for Well-Being by Stewart B. Nuland. Random House, New York (2007). Although the book contains chapters on the physical side of aging, of being stricken with unfortunate conditions, of facing loss and decline, each chapter also details case studies in which the overpowering message is that no condition is essentially filled with doom.

Faith in the Future: Healthcare, Aging, and the Role of Religion by Harold G. Koenig and Douglas M. Lawson. Templeton Foundation Press, Radnor, PA (2004). The authors believe a major role for the church is to train volunteer caregivers and other volunteers to interact with the growing numbers of older adults.

Healthy Aging: A Lifelong Guide to Your Physical and Spiritual Well-Being by Andrew Weil, M.D. Alfred A. Knopf, New York (2005). This book suggests that although aging is an irreversible process, there are myriad things we can do to keep our minds and bodies in good working order through all phases of life.

Is Religion Good for Your Health? The Effects of Religion on Physical and Mental Health by Harold G. Koenig, M.D. Haworth Press, New York (1997). The research found in this resource suggests that there is a relationship between religion and good physical and mental health.

Successful Aging: The MacArthur Foundation Study by John W. Rowe, M.D. and Robert L. Kahn, Ph.D. Random House, Inc., New York, NY (1998). A good book about lifestyle choices which, according to the authors, are more important than genes, in determining how well we age.

Chapter 3: Retirement and Aging

Beyond the Myths and Magic of Mentoring (Revised Edition) by M. Murray and M.A. Owen. Sand Francisco: Jossey-Bass, 2001. This helpful resource provides the reader with advice, tools, and case studies needed to harness the power of mentoring.

Comfort Zones: Planning a Fulfilling Retirement (5th Edition) by Marion E. Haynes. Crisp Learning (2005). This resource brings together all the major aspects of retirement, including relationships, health issues, use of time, living arrangements, finances and more.

The Complete Guide to Creative Retirement by Rob Kelley. Turnkey Press, Austin, TX (2003). This resource helps guide older adults in exploring issues of self reinvention.

The Creative Age: Awakening Human Potential in the Second Half of Life by Gene D. Cohen, M.D., Ph.D. Quill/Harper Collins, New York (2001) This resource helps debunk the harmful myths about aging and illuminates the biological and emotional foundations for creativity.

Musical Chairs: One Man's Quest to Find Meaning in the Second Half of Life (video) Church Health, Edmonds, WA (2006) A short video useful for discussion and small groups exploring meaning and purpose in retirement. See also website at www.chonline.org

The New Retirement: The Ultimate Guide to the Rest of Your Life by Jan Cullinane and Cathy Fitzgerald. Rodale Books (2004). A comprehensive guide to facing decisions related to work, money, health care, lifestyle, and more.

Purpose and Power in Retirement: New Opportunities for Meaning and Purpose by Harold G. Koenig, M.D. Templeton Foundation Press (2005). Book and Audio CD. This resource encourages retirees to make a meaningful difference in the world.

Settling In: My First Year in a Retirement Community by Richard H. Morgan. Upper Room Books, Nashville, TN (2006). Through Scripture, prayers, and brief meditations, Morgan addresses the fears of the retirement years including loss of health, loss of cognitive ability, and loss of social status.

Chapter 4: Spirituality and Aging

Aging and Spirituality: Spiritual Dimensions of Aging Theory, Research, Practice, and Policy by David O. Moberg. Haworth Pastoral Press, Binghamton, NY (2001). This resource provides valuable information for clergy and other professionals in understanding and helping older adults experience spiritual awakening and discovery in the later years.

Aging, Spirituality, and Religion edited by Melvin A. Kimble, Susan H. McFadden, and all. Fortress Press, Minneapolis, MN (1995). Volume 1. This book examines the ways religion and spirituality are experienced by aging persons within an aging society.

Aging, Spirituality, and Religion, Volume 2 edited by Melvin A. Kimble and Susan H. McFadden. Fortress Press, Minneapolis, MN (2003). Picking up where Volume 1 left off, this book contains substantive theoretical essays on how religion and spirituality are encountered in the growth experiences and life crises of older adults.

The Art of Growing Old by Carroll Saussy. Augsburg, Minneapolis, MN (1998). A helpful guide for older adults who want to fully engage in the possibilities of creativity and depth of soul in the later years.

Autumn Wisdom: Finding Meaning in the Autumn of Your Life by Jim Miller. Augsburg Fortress, Minneapolis, MN (1995). A valuable resource designed to be read slowly and reflectively for older adults who are searching for deeper meaning in their later years.

A Deepening Love Affair: The Gift of God in Later Life by Jane Marie Thibault. Upper Room Books, Nashville, TN (1993). A classic book on spirituality in life's later years and ways to become aware of our gifts.

From Age-ing to Sage-ing: A Profound New Vision of Growing Older by Zalman Schachter-Shalomi and Ronald S. Miller. Warner Books, Inc., New York (1995). This valuable resource invites older adults to harness the power of God's spirit and to use one's experiences to nurture and help younger generations.

Gaining a Heart of Wisdom: Finding Meaning in the Autumn of Your Life (Video). An inspiring video, enhanced by beautiful photography, that invites older adults to find meaning in their later years. Willowgreen, Fort Worth, IN. (36 minutes)

Growing Old in Christ edited by Stanley Hauerwas, Carole Bailey Stoneking, Keith G. Meador, and David Cloutier. Eerdmans Publishing, Grand Rapid, MI (2003). Presents a serious theological reflection on what it means to grow old.

Living with Purpose in a Worn-Out Body: Spiritual Encouragement for Older Adults by Missy Buchanan. Upper Room Books, Nashville (2008).

Reflections on Aging and Spiritual Growth by Andrew J. Weaver, Harold G. Koenig, and Phyllis C. Roe. Abingdon Press, Nashville, TN (1998). Twelve stories about men and women who have experienced spiritual growth in the later years.

Remembering Your Story: A Guide to Spiritual Autobiography by Richard L. Morgan. Upper Room Books, Nashville, TN (2002). Designed for small groups, this resource encourages and guides participants through 10 sessions of life review and future direction.

Rock of Ages: A Worship and Songbook for Retirement Living. Discipleship Resources, Nashville, TN (2002). A large print worship and songbook for older adults.

Senior Spirituality by Harold R. Nelson. Chalice Press, St. Louis, MO (2004). This book addresses the relationship between spirituality and life's adversity, creativity and healing, and grief and loss.

10 Gospel Promises for Later Life by Jane Marie Thibault. Upper Room Books, Nashville (2004). This helpful resource invites readers to identify their own fears and learn to make the most of God's gift of longer life.

Winter Grace: Spirituality and Aging by Kathleen Fischer. Upper Room Books, Nashville (1998). A classic book showing how the losses that accompany aging can lead to freedom and new life.

Chapter 5: Caregiving and Aging

Building a Ministry for Homebound and Nursing Home Residents by Marie White Webb. Discipleship Resources, Nashville, TN (2003). An excellent guidebook for doing ministry with homebound and residents in continuing care retirement communities.

The Caregiver's Book: Caring for Another, Caring for Yourself by James E. Miller. Willowgreen, Fort Wayne, IN. This resource explores the caregiver's role, feelings, and experiences.

The Complete Eldercare Planner by Joy Loverde. Three Rivers Press, New York (2000). A comprehensive resource on eldercare and caregiving issues.

From Grim to Green Pastures: Meditations for the Sick and Their Caregivers by Richard L. Morgan. Upper Room Books, Nashville, TN (1994). A valuable resource for for who are ill and those who care for them.

How to Care for Aging Parents by Virginia Morris. Workman Publishing,

New York (1996). This resource addresses issues involved in caring for aging parents including medical, emotional, legal, and financial concerns.

A Ministry of Caring by Duane A. Ewers. Discipleship Resources, Nashville, TN. A skill training course divided into 11 sessions for helping laity in a ministry of caring. There is both a leader's guide and a participant's workbook.

Parish Nursing: Promoting Whole Person Health Within Faith Communities edited by Phyllis Ann Solari-Twadell and Mary Ann McDermott. Sage Publications, Thousand Oaks, CA (1999). A valuable resource that provides not only an overview of parish nurse ministry but helpful suggestions for establishing such a powerful ministry.

Pastoral Care of Older Adults by Harold G. Koenig and Andrew J. Weaver. Fortress Press, Minneapolis, MN (1998). This book provides practical guidance for pastors in their caregiving ministry with aging and older adults.

With God's Oldest Friends: Pastoral Visiting in the Nursing Home by Henry C. Simmons and Mark A. Peters. Wipf & Stock, Eugene, OR (2003). A valuable resource for caregiving in nursing home settings.

When You're the Caregiver: 12 Things to Do If Someone You Care For Is Ill or Incapacitated by James E. Miller. Willowgreen, Fort Wayne, IN. This resource provides the caregiver with 12 practical, affirming ideas to help deliver the best possible assistance to those being cared for.

Chapter 6: Death and Aging

And Not One Bird Stopped Singing: Coping with Transition and Loss in Aging by Doris Moreland Jones. Upper Room Books, Nashville, TN (1997). This helpful resource guides the reader facing various losses and transitions including coping with the death of a spouse.

Dying Well: Peace and Possibilities at the End of Life by Ira Byock. Riverhead Books, New York, NY (1997). This book and website www.dyingwell.com make an essential contribution to understanding death and its implications for ministry.

Five Wishes by Aging with Dignity, Tallahassee, FL (www.agingwithdignity .org) This resource booklet gives people a way to control how they want to be treated when they become seriously ill and what they want loved ones to know.

Living Fully, Dying Well by Bishop Rueben P. Job. Abingdon Press, Nashville, TN (2006). This study which contains a leader's guide, participant workbook, and video is designed to assist people in making careful, wise, and prayerful preparation for meeting life's most important moments.

Mrs. Hunter's Happy Death: Lessons on Living From People Preparing to Die by John Fanestil. Doubleday (2006) A unique, uplifting, and timely book dealing with dying and death.

Tuesdays with Morrie: an Old Man, a Young Man, and Life's Greatest Lesson by Mitch Albom. Doubleday (1997). The true story about the relationship between a spiritual mentor and pupil as they confront aging, dying, and death.

Chapter 7: Ministry and Aging

Adult Ministries: Guidelines for Leading Your Congregation by Richard H. Gentzler, Jr., Debra Smith, and Bill Lizor. Cokesbury, Nashville, TN (2008). A "how-to" guide, providing practical ideas and models for adult ministry (including older adult ministry) in congregational settings.

Amazing Grays: Unleashing the Power of Age in Your Congregation by Leona and Richard Bergstrom. Church Health, Edmonds, WA (2000). This resource helps congregations tap into the wealth of wisdom and experience of older adults in the congregation. See also website at www.chonline.org

Designing an Older Adult Ministry by Richard H. Gentzler, Jr. Discipleship Resources, Nashville, TN (1999). A "how-to" and informative resource for organizing and sustaining an intentional ministry by, with, and for older adults in local church settings.

Dimensions of Older Adult Ministry: A Handbook edited by Richard L. Morgan. Witherspoon Press, Presbyterian Church (USA), Louisville, KY (2006). This resource provides basic information necessary for understanding the aging process and older people.

Engaging in Ministry with Older Adults by Dosia Carlson. Alban Institute, Bethesda, MD (1997). A helpful and practical book describing various models for older adult ministry.

The Graying of the Church: A Leader's Guide to Older Adult Ministry in The United Methodist Church by Richard H. Gentzler, Jr. Discipleship Resources, Nashville, TN (2004). Valuable information about aging in our society and in the church: who are they, what do they believe, how are they motivated, and what resources are available?

How To Minister Among Older Adults by Charles T. Knippel. Concordia Publishing House, St. Louis, MO (2005). This manual explores the many options for ministry with and to the older adult age group. Also included are planning forms to start or expand an older adult ministry program.

How To Say It to Seniors: Closing the Communication Gap with Our Elders by David Solie, M.S., P.A. Prentice Hall Press, New York (2004). This resource provides valuable information on how to remove the typical communication blocks we have with the elderly.

A Journey Called Aging: Challenges and Opportunities in Older Adulthood by James C. Fisher and Henry C. Simmons. Haworth Press, Binghamton, NY (2007). A useful resource in helping older adults plan their own "journey" through the later years.

Ministering to Older Adults: The Building Blocks, edited by Donald R. Koepke. Haworth Press, Binghamton, NY (2005). This resource provides a step-by-step approach for designing a congregational based ministry with older adults.

Ministry to and with the Elderly by Timothy M. Farabaugh. Authorhouse, Bloomington, IN (2005). A resource that not only provides information about the unique needs of older adults but provides examples and ways both clergy and elderly may be involved in ministry with older adults.

Our Help In Ages Past: The Black Church's Ministry Among the Elderly by Bobby Joe Saucer with Jean Alicia Elster. Judson Press, Valley Forge, PA (2005). This resource challenges and engages black churches (Baptist) in developing intentional ministry among older adults.

Senior Adult Ministry in the 21ˢᵗ Century by David P. Gallagher. Group, Loveland, CO (2002). This helpful resource provides step-by-step strategies for reaching people over 50 years of age.

Chapter 8: Boomers and Aging

Celebrating the Rest of Your Life: A Baby Boomer's Guide to Spirituality by David Yount. Augsburg Books, Minneapolis, MN (2005) A valuable resource to help Boomers find meaning and satisfaction in the retirement years.

Forty-Sixty: A Study for Midlife Adults Who Want to Make a Difference by Richard H. Gentzler, Jr. and Craig Kennet Miller. Discipleship Resources, Nashville, TN (2001). A small group study book for Baby Boomers and midlife adults who are personally confronting the many issues of aging.

The Greater Generation: In Defense of the Baby Boom Legacy by Leonard Steinhorn. Thomas Dunne Books, St. Martin's Press, New York (2006). This resource provides insight into the values and complexity of Baby Boomers and the important role they play in shaping America.

Marketing to Leading-Edge Baby Boomers by Brent Green. Paramount Market Publishing, Ithaca, NY (2005). This resource provides valuable information and insight for congregational leaders who are seeking to reach Baby Boomers.

The Power Years: A User's Guide to the Rest of Your Life by Ken Dychtwald & Daniel Kadlec, John Wiley & Sons, Inc., Hoboken, NJ (2005). A guidebook to help midlife and older adults realize their potential by redefining expectations.

Primetime: How Baby Boomers will Revolutionize Retirement and Change America by Marc Freedman. Public Affairs, New York (1999). The author depicts an explosion of possibility for communities, for older people, for children, for American society.

Spiritual Marketplace: Baby Boomers and the Remaking of American Religion by Wade Clark Roof. Princeton University Press, Princeton, NJ (1999). This resource identifies the religious and spiritual styles, family patterns, and moral vision and values of Boomers.

Adult Faith Journey

Our spirituality encompasses all that we are and do. It is living with the ordinary and commonplace things in life, and being open and ready to find God there. Such living elicits trust, awe, and wonder in us. It brings us to a sense of faithfulness that can be described as "turning one's heart toward God."

Faith experiences begin early and continue throughout life. They tell of struggles and new beginnings—of a relationship between God and the believer that is gathered up in a story, *our* story of a faith journey.

Faith experiences cannot be contained in educational institutions or curriculum materials. Faith is always embodied and modeled in the lives of those who, whether for good or ill, teach us. If teachers want to nurture the faith of others, they need to nurture their own faith, becoming more and more conscious of what they are modeling to learners.

Using the timeline below, draw simple lifeline for yourself. Start it wherever you wish and bring it up to the present. In a word or two identify high and low points on your lifeline.

Now draw in a different color or as a dotted line a faithline over the lifeline. Think of these questions as you identify the highs and lows of your faithline:

> When you have sensed the movement
> of the Holy Spirit in your life?

> When have you felt God at a distance?

+

Birth _____

5   10   15   20   25   30   35   40   45   50   55   60   65   70   75   80   85

Chronological Age

−

S.E.N.I.O.R.S. Ministry Grid

Local Church Assessment

Biblical Foundation: "For this reason we never become discouraged. Even though our physical being is gradually decaying, yet our spiritual being is renewed day by day." (2 Corinthians 4:16)

Purpose: The purpose of older adult ministry is to make disciples of Jesus Christ: to nurture faith, build Christian community, and equip seniors for faithful living and service.

S.E.N.I.O.R.S. Ministry Assessment	Active Phase Go–Go's	Passive Phase Slow–Go's	Final Phase No–Go's
Spirituality			
Enrichment			
Nutrition/Wellness			
Intergenerational			
Outreach			
Recreation			
Service			

Older Adult Survey—Sample 1

Name:_____

Address:_____

_____

Phone #:_____ Email Address:_____

Gender: ☐ Female   ☐ Male   Date of Birth:_____

Marital Status: ☐ Married, ☐ Single, ☐ Never Married, ☐ Divorced, ☐ Widowed

Do you live alone? ☐ Yes ☐ No
If No, with whom do you live?_____

In the event of an emergency, if you need help or became ill or disabled, is there someone to whom you could turn for assistance? ☐ Yes ☐ No

If Yes, who?_____ Relationship:_____

Address:_____ Telephone #_____

During the past week, how many times did you:
Have someone visit you? _____ Visit someone else? _____
Go shopping? _____ Talk with a friend or relative on the telephone? _____

Do you experience any problems with where you live? ☐ Yes ☐ No

If Yes, what are the problems?_____

Please rate your health: ☐ Excellent ☐ Very Good ☐ Good ☐ Fair ☐ Poor

Approximately how often do you attend religious services?
☐ Weekly ☐ Twice a month ☐ Monthly ☐ Quarterly ☐ Yearly ☐ Never

Would you like to receive any of the following religious services in your home?

☐ Pastoral Visitation ☐ Lay Visitation ☐ Devotional materials
☐ Bible Study materials ☐ Holy Communion ☐ Worship Service tapes
☐ Other, please specify:_____

(Check all that are appropriate)

Do You Need?		Can You Provide?
☐Yes ☐ No	Transportation	☐Yes ☐ No
☐Yes ☐ No	Home Repairs	☐Yes ☐ No
☐Yes ☐ No	Housekeeping Chores	☐Yes ☐ No
☐Yes ☐ No	Minor Plumbing Repairs	☐Yes ☐ No
☐Yes ☐ No	Minor Carpentry Repairs	☐Yes ☐ No
☐Yes ☐ No	Legal Counsel	☐Yes ☐ No
☐Yes ☐ No	Income Tax Preparation	☐Yes ☐ No
☐Yes ☐ No	Financial Counsel	☐Yes ☐ No
☐Yes ☐ No	Medical Assistance	☐Yes ☐ No
☐Yes ☐ No	Meal Preparation	☐Yes ☐ No
☐Yes ☐ No	Reading Materials	☐Yes ☐ No
☐Yes ☐ No	Support Group	☐Yes ☐ No
☐Yes ☐ No	Fellowship Group	☐Yes ☐ No
☐Yes ☐ No	Bible Study Group	☐Yes ☐ No
☐Yes ☐ No	Prayer Group	☐Yes ☐ No
☐Yes ☐ No	Caregivers Support Group	☐Yes ☐ No
☐Yes ☐ No	Respite Support	☐Yes ☐ No
☐Yes ☐ No	Travel Opportunities	☐Yes ☐ No

Other Need(s) You Have: _____

_____

_____

Other Ministry You Can Provide:_____

_____

_____

Please identify or list any programs the church (or seniors group) should provide for older persons:_____

Name of Interviewer:_____ Date:_____

Older Adult Survey—Sample 2

Section I: Contact Information

Interviewer: _____

Date of Interview: _____

Name of Member being interviewed: _____

Address of Member: _____

_____

Telephone # of Member: _____ Email Address: _____

1. Age: _____   2. Birthdate: Mo__ __ Day__ __ Yr__ __ __ __

3. Gender: Female __ Male __   4. Race/Ethnicity: _____

Did other(s) participate in interview or speak for member? ___Yes ___ No

(If Yes) Name: _____ Relationship: _____

Section II: Life Story

5. Invite Member to share aspects of his/her life: _____

_____

_____

_____

_____

_____

_____

_____

Section III: Current Demographics

6. Living Arrangement:

_____ Independent w/spouse in own home
_____ Independent alone in own home
_____ With children in their home
_____ In communal setting
_____ Assisted-living facility
_____ Hospital/Nursing Home
_____ Other: _____

7. Mobility Status: Go-Go _____   Slow-Go _____   No-Go _____

Explain: _____

_____

Section IV: Attitudes, Interests & Opinions

8. What could your church offer to make your life better?

A. _____
B. _____
C. _____
D. _____

9. What things do you like most to do that bring joy to your life?

_____

_____

_____

10. Is the church doing enough of the right things to serve needs of older members?

_____

_____

_____

Interviewer post-interview comments and observations: _____

_____

_____

_____

APPENDIX E

Generational Anchor Points

For Older Adults and "Leading Edge" Boomers

(Shared values and events that affect youth and young adults and help define or shape an age cohort throughout life)

	GI Generation Born: 1905-1925 Wars: World War II (The Big War)	Silent or Swing 1926-1945 Korean War (The Forgotten War)	"Leading Edge" Boomers 1946-1954 Vietnam War (The Protested War)
Outlook:	Conformists	Conciliatory/Mediators Facilitators	Individualists "Me" Generation
Economics:	Builders/Problem Solvers Depression	Rising Affluence	Prosperity
Money:	Save	Save & Spend	Spend
Family:	Large Extended	Extended	Nuclear
Technology:	Radio LP Records Operator-Assisted Phone	B&W TV Reel to Reel Tape Rotary Phone	Color TV/VCR 8 Track/Cassette Tapes Touchtone Phone
Presidents:	FDR	Truman/Eisenhower	JFK/Johnson/Nixon
Music:	Big Band	Swing	Rock'n'Roll
Lifestyle:	Prohibition	Alcohol/Cigarettes	Marijuana/LSD
Sex:	Taboo	Early Marriages	Sexual Revolution
Living:	Farm Life	City/Towns	Suburbs
Drinks:	Coffee	Instant Coffee	Cola/Soft Drink
Religion:	"Mainline" Protestant	Rising Catholic Influence	"New Age" & Cults

©Information: Adult Ministries by Richard H. Gentzler, Jr., D.Min., Director, Center on Aging and Older Adult Ministries, P.O. Box 340003, Nashville, TN 37203-0003 Tele: (877) 899-2780 x 7173, Fax: (615) 340-7071. (Developed from the idea of "Generational Markers" found in Rocking the Ages: The Yankelovich Report on Generational Marketing by J. Walker Smith and Ann Clurman. HarperBusiness, 1997)

About the Author

A native of York, Pennsylvania, Dr. Richard H. Gentzler, Jr. (Rick) is director of the Center on Aging and Older Adult Ministries for the General Board of Discipleship of The United Methodist Church in Nashville, TN. As a much sought after speaker and seminar leader, Dr. Gentzler is nationally recognized as a teacher, writer, and leader in the field of aging and older adult ministries.

In addition to ***Aging & Ministry in the 21st Century: An Inquiry Approach***, Dr. Gentzler is the author and co-author of numerous other books on aging and older adult ministry, including: ***The Graying of the Church: A Leader's Guide for Older Adult Ministry in The United Methodist Church***; ***Designing an Older Adult Ministry***; ***Aging: God's Challenge to Church and Synagogue***; ***Forty-Sixty: A Guide for Midlife Adults Who Want to Make a Difference***; ***Adult Ministries (***Guidelines for Leading Your Congregation series***)***; ***1999 International Year of Older Persons: Resource Materials for Congregational Ministry with Older Adults***; ***The Pulse of United Methodist Baby Boomers***; and, ***Rock of Ages*** (a large print worship and song book). In 2003 he received the National Interfaith Coalition on Aging (NICA) "Spirituality and Aging" Award and in 2005 he helped produce an award winning video on aging and older adult ministries titled, ***New Beginnings: The Gifts of Aging***.

Prior to joining the staff at the General Board of Discipleship, Dr. Gentzler served as pastor of several United Methodist congregations in Pennsylvania and Maryland. He also served as chaplain in various nursing home settings and developed a chaplaincy services program while working on his doctorate at Boston University School of Theology. He taught in various undergraduate degree programs and is presently an adjunct faculty member at Wesley Theological Seminary in Washington, DC, where he teaches various courses on aging and older adult ministries.

Dr. Gentzler received a Bachelor of Science in Education degree from Shippensburg University (Shippensburg, PA), a Master of Divinity degree from Wesley Theological Seminary (Washington, DC), and a Doctor of Ministry degree from Boston University School of Theology (Boston, MA).